Evidence-Based Practice Model for Youth with Externalizing Disorders

Kirstin Painter

Evidence-Based Practice Model for Youth with Externalizing Disorders

Multisystemic Therapy

LAP LAMBERT Academic Publishing

Impressum/Imprint (nur für Deutschland/ only for Germany)

Bibliografische Information der Deutschen Nationalbibliothek: Die Deutsche Nationalbibliothek verzeichnet diese Publikation in der Deutschen Nationalbibliografie; detaillierte bibliografische Daten sind im Internet über http://dnb.d-nb.de abrufbar.

Alle in diesem Buch genannten Marken und Produktnamen unterliegen warenzeichen-, marken- oder patentrechtlichem Schutz bzw. sind Warenzeichen oder eingetragene Warenzeichen der jeweiligen Inhaber. Die Wiedergabe von Marken, Produktnamen, Gebrauchsnamen, Handelsnamen, Warenbezeichnungen u.s.w. in diesem Werk berechtigt auch ohne besondere Kennzeichnung nicht zu der Annahme, dass solche Namen im Sinne der Warenzeichen- und Markenschutzgesetzgebung als frei zu betrachten wären und daher von jedermann benutzt werden dürften.

Coverbild: www.purestockx.com

Verlag: LAP LAMBERT Academic Publishing AG & Co. KG
Theodor-Heuss-Ring 26, 50668 Köln, Germany
Telefon: +49 681 3720-310, Telefax: +49 681 3720-3109, Email: info@lap-publishing.com

Herstellung in Deutschland:
Schaltungsdienst Lange o.H.G., Berlin
Books on Demand GmbH, Norderstedt
Reha GmbH, Saarbrücken
Amazon Distribution GmbH, Leipzig
ISBN: 978-3-8383-0253-9

Imprint (only for USA, GB)

Bibliographic information published by the Deutsche Nationalbibliothek: The Deutsche Nationalbibliothek lists this publication in the Deutsche Nationalbibliografie; detailed bibliographic data are available in the Internet at http://dnb.d-nb.de.

Any brand names and product names mentioned in this book are subject to trademark, brand or patent protection and are trademarks or registered trademarks of their respective holders. The use of brand names, product names, common names, trade names, product descriptions etc. even without a particular marking in this works is in no way to be construed to mean that such names may be regarded as unrestricted in respect of trademark and brand protection legislation and could thus be used by anyone.

Cover image: www.purestockx.com

Publisher:
LAP LAMBERT Academic Publishing AG & Co. KG
Theodor-Heuss-Ring 26, 50668 Köln, Germany
Phone: +49 681 3720-310, Fax: +49 681 3720-3109, Email: info@lap-publishing.com

Printed in the U.S.A.
Printed in the U.K. by (see last page)
ISBN: 978-3-8383-0253-9

TABLE OF CONTENTS

Chapter

LIST OF TABLES

CHAPTER 1

STATEMENT OF THE PROBLEM

<u>1.1 Introduction</u>

Mental illness is serious public health problem that goes largely unrecognized

by many Americans. Mental illness is the number one cause of disability in the United

States and costs the US approximately $79 billion due to a loss of productivity,

incarcerations, and mortality costs (New Freedom Commission, 2003). In 2003, the

President's New Freedom Commission reported children's mental health to be public

health crises in the United States, reporting many barriers exist that impede children

from receiving appropriate mental health care. These barriers include a fragmented

service delivery system, stigma, financial barriers, and a lag between discovery of

effective treatments and the time it takes to put them into practice. This is quite

disturbing as an estimated 1 in 10 children and adolescents in the United States suffer

from a serious mental illness resulting in significant impairments across all aspects of

their lives (National Advisory Mental Health Council Workgroup on Child and

Adolescent Mental Health Intervention Development and Deployment, 2001). Further,

children's mental health problems are becoming increasingly more complex. Over

380,000 children are diagnosed with multiple mental health problems (Pottick &

Warner, 2003). The most problematic disorders of childhood are externalizing disorders

such as attention deficit hyperactivity disorder (ADHD), oppositional defiant disorder

1

(ODD), and conduct disorder (CD) due to their high prevalence and association with difficulties in adulthood such as criminal activity, unemployment, substance abuse, inadequate parenting, and relationship problems (Farmer, Compton, Burns, & Robertson, 2002).

Youth with externalizing disorders often exhibit negative moods, problems adapting, inflexibility, difficulty managing behavior, high reactivity, high irritability, and high intensity (Stormont, 2002). Due to these problem behaviors and poor coping, they often experience relationship problems with peers, teachers, and family; problems in school; difficulty solving problems; difficulty coping; and low self esteem (Henggeler, Rodick, Borduin, Hanson, Watson, & Urey, 1986). Youth with externalizing disorders often have experienced physical abuse, neglect, poverty, and or family dysfunction leading to their disorder (Schoenwald & Rowland, 2002). They often have caregivers with parenting styles which are punitive or neglectful (Campbell & Ewing, 1990) and who have psychopathologic behavior of their own (Pfiffner, McBurnett, Lahey, Frick, Loeber, Green, & Rathouz, 1999). They often live in neighborhoods with high crime, high violence, and lack of opportunity to participate in pro-social activities (Henggeler, Schoenwald et al., 2002). Left untreated, these externalizing disorders can develop into psychopathological behavior and chronic delinquency that will disrupt positive development and follow them into adulthood (Bergman & Magnusson, 1997; Farmer et al, 2002; Hill, Coie, Lochman, & Greenberg, 2004). In order to adequately intervene in these problems, we must not only treat the youth, but we must intervene in all areas contributing to the problem behavior. If we

2

remove youth from their natural environment and only treat the youth, they are more likely to recidivate back to prior problem behavior when returned to their natural environment due to our not intervening in all areas of the environment contributing to the externalizing disorder. (A more in-depth discussion on the correlates of externalizing disorders will be discussed in section 2.2.1.)

According to the New Freedom Commission report (2003), gaps of knowledge exist of effective, culturally competent, community-based services for children and adolescents with serious emotional disturbance. Further, there is great disparity between the evidence-base of effective community-based treatments for youth with mental health disorders and the treatments that are available to them (Weisz, 2000). Untreated or inadequately treated youth are likely to end up in the child welfare or juvenile justice systems, particularly those with externalizing disorders (Texas Institute for Policy Research, 2005). Nearly half the children in the child welfare system have serious emotional or behavioral needs (Burns, Phillips, Wagner, Barth, Kolko, Campbell, & Landsverk, 2004; Scannapieco & Connell-Carrick, 2005); and, the rates of youth with mental health problems in the juvenile justice system have been found to be much higher than that of the general population (Coalition for Juvenile Justice, n.d.; Waxman & Collins, 2004). An estimated 36% of youth involved in the juvenile system nationally became involved due to inadequate or unavailable mental health services (Mental Health Association in Texas, 2005). According to the U.S. General Accounting Office, 12,700 families relinquished custody of their children in 2003 in order to receive mental health treatment. It is imperative to address mental health issues of youth in order to

3

prevent and reduce future delinquency (Wasserman, Ko, & Mc Reynolds, 2004) and prevent future problems in adulthood (Farmer et al., 2002).

Not providing appropriate mental health services to youth can have profound consequences as untreated or under-treated mental health problems disrupt children's development, sometimes permanently (Pottick & Warner, 2003). Children of color living in poverty are at a higher risk of not receiving appropriate, adequate care than other youth (Gonzales, 2005). It is estimated that 79 % of youth with mental health problems do not receive the care they need (Dabahnah & Cooper, 2006). Seriously emotionally disturbed children not receiving appropriate mental health services typically experience poor school performance, poor peer relationships, and poor family relationships (Pottick & Warner, 2003). Again, as adults, they typically go on to experience problems with relationships and employment, and are less likely to complete school (Pottick & Warner, 2003).

The research on effective treatment for children with mental health disorders has greatly expanded over the past several years. However, the vast amount of research has *not* been conducted in the home and community setting where children reside (Burns, Hoagwood, & Mrazek, 1999) or with multi-problem youth and families (Evidence-based Services Committee Biennial Report, 2004). The typical child or adolescent presenting to community mental health centers often present with a higher co-morbidity and greater clinical severity of symptoms than youth in clinical trials (Weisz, Huey & Weersing, 1998). Little empirical research exists on interventions addressing co-morbidity or that combine treatments to address the multiple antecedents of mental health (Zaff, Calkins, Bridges, & Margie, 2002).

Three integrated service modalities for treating youth with a severe emotional disturbance examined in the literature are intensive case management, treatment foster care, and home-based services (Burns et al., 1999; Burns & Hoagwood, 2002; Hoagwood, 2001). Case management research is very limited and has mixed results. Currently, four randomized controlled studies exist of case management (Burns, Farmer, Angold, Costello, & Behar, 1996; Cauce & Morgan, 1994; Evans & Armstrong, 1994; Evans & Boothroyd, 1997). There is evidence across the studies of a decrease in youth psychiatric symptoms, a decrease in behavioral problems, and improvement in youth functioning; however, due to the variance between study designs and the small number of studies, it is difficult to draw any strong conclusions about the effectiveness of intensive case management. Though treatment foster care research looks promising, youth are placed in foster care homes for treatment, thus removing them from their natural environment and placing them in a more restrictive setting (Craven & Lee, 2006). Much of the research on home-based services has been sponsored through the juvenile justice (Multisystemic Therapy) or child welfare systems (family preservation) rather than through the mental health system (U.S. Department of Health and Human Services, 1999). While family preservation has been shown to be helpful with some youth and families, it has not been shown to be effective with multi-problem families (Lindsey, Martin, & Doh, 2002). Youth and families in the community mental health system tend to be multi-problem families. Clearly, evidence-based treatment models provided in the home and community are needed to treat this

5

population of youth and their multi-problem families.

Of all the service modalities, Multisystemic Therapy (MST) stands out as a culturally competent family and home-based service with strong empirical evidence for treating certain populations in the juvenile justice system (Burns et al., 1999), emerging evidence of effectiveness in the child welfare system (Burns et al., 1999), and may have promise for treating youth with a serious emotional disturbance, particularly those with externalizing disorders, in the community mental health system. MST was conceived to treat juvenile offenders and has been tested with some of the most challenging youth to treat in the juvenile justice system (Evidence-based Services Committee, 2004). It has achieved favorable long-term outcomes such as reduced out-of-home placement, increased school attendance, and cost savings for youth presenting with serious clinical problems (e.g., violence, substance abuse, serious mental health treatment needs) (Henggeler, 2003). To date, two studies exist on the use of MST with non-juveniles with a severe emotional disturbance (Henggeler, Rowland, Halliday-Boykins, Sheidow, Ward, Randall, Pickrel, Cunningham & Edwards, 2003; Rowland, Halliday-Boykins, Henggeler, Cunningham, Lee, Kruesi, & Shapiro, 2005). Results of both studies were favorable with MST outcomes (see Chapter 3).

MST is considered an evidence-based program (Evidence-based Services Committee, 2004). It has been recognized as a Model Program by the Substance Abuse and Mental Health Services Administration and the Office of Juvenile Justice and Delinquency Prevention, an Effective Program by the U.S. Surgeon General's Report on Mental Health and Youth Violence, and is recipient of the *Families Count* Award by

6

the Annie E. Casey Foundation. In order to be considered evidence-based, a treatment must be found superior to another treatment modality through randomized, controlled studies that have been replicated (Wasserman, Ko, & Jenson, 2001). Whereas some agree MST is a well validated, evidence-based program for the treatment of juvenile offenders, including those with mental health or substance abuse disorders (Burns & Friedman, 1990; Henggeler, Schoenwald, Borduin, Rowland & Cunningham, 1998; Hoagwood, Burns, Kiser, Ringeisen, & Schoenwald, 2001; Kazdin & Weisz, 1998); others are questioning its true efficacy due to most empirical studies being conducted by MST program developers (Littell, Popa, & Forsythe, 2005).

1.2 Purpose of Study

The purpose of this study was to evaluate the use of MST with seriously emotionally disturbed youth in a community mental health setting. This study compared multisystemic therapy to *usual services* for seriously emotionally disturbed youth with externalizing disorders. Usual services consisted of intensive case management and parent skills training using *Defiant Teen* (Barkley, Edward, & Robin, 1999) or *Defiant Children* (Barkley, 1997). Barkley (1997) developed the curriculums based on research which supports each procedure utilized throughout the manuals. Both MST and usual services were provided in the home and community of the youth.

This population was chosen because youth with a severe emotional disturbance without juvenile justice involvement made up 37% of youth served by TDMHMR as identified in a cluster analyses of youth served under the Texas Department of Mental Health and Mental Retardation in FY2001 and FY2002 (Hoagwood, 2003). Of the

7

youth identified, 54% were diagnosed with ADHD and 39% with Conduct Disorder. The total average Axis I diagnoses for this group was 1.73. The average age was 11.7 years old. This group was also found to have a high level of acting out behaviors (externalizing behaviors), family problems, and school problems. In comparison, youth identified in the *Juvenile Justice Cluster* in the TDMHMR cluster analysis had an average age of 15.3 and an average of 1.89 Axis I diagnoses. MST research has been shown to improve acting out behavior of youth, family problems, and school problems (Henggeler et al., 1998). Effective mental health treatment has been shown to reduce future crime (Rice & Miller, 1999; as cited by Texas Institute for Health Policy Research and United Ways of Texas, 2003). Because youth in the SED cluster experienced similar problems to those in the juvenile justice cluster, but had not reached the point of juvenile justice involvement, it is felt that intervening in these problems earlier might improve mental health functioning and prevent youth from becoming involved in the juvenile justice system.

This was an important study in that it compared MST to other treatments with some empirical support (case management and Barkley's skills training) occurring in the community, thus contributing to a need to enhance research knowledge through comparing different credible treatments to one another (Jensen, Weersing, Hoagwood & Goldman, 2005). Further, this study sought to fill a gap that exists in the empirical literature for youth with serious emotional disturbance in community mental health. The need for increased research conducted in the natural environment of children and adolescents with serious emotional impairments further strengthens the importance of this study as the treatments being studied occurred in the homes and communities in which the youth reside. Finally, due to current questions regarding all but one existing MST study being conducted by a founder of MST, having a study of MST conducted by an entity not connected to MST services further strengthened this study's importance. This study contributed to this body of knowledge through testing the following research hypotheses.

1.3 Research Hypotheses

1.3.1 Overarching Research Hypothesis

Emotionally disturbed youth in a community mental health setting who have a mental health Axis I externalizing disorder that receive multisystemic therapy will experience more improved treatment outcomes than those receiving usual community services.

1.3.2 Secondary Research Hypotheses

1a. Emotionally disturbed youth in a community mental health setting with a mental health Axis I externalizing disorder who receive multisystemic therapy will experience more improved mental health symptoms than those receiving usual community services.

1b. Emotionally disturbed youth in a community mental health setting with a mental health Axis I externalizing disorder who receive multisystemic therapy will experience more improved functioning than those receiving usual community services.

9

1c. Emotionally disturbed youth in a community mental health setting with a mental health Axis I externalizing disorder who receive multisystemic therapy will experience more improved school behavior than those receiving usual community services.

1d. Emotionally disturbed youth in a community mental health setting with a mental health Axis I externalizing disorder who receive multisystemic therapy will experience more improved family functioning than those receiving usual community services.

1e. Emotionally disturbed youth in a community mental health setting with a mental health Axis I externalizing disorder who receive multisystemic therapy will experience decreased risk of self harm than those receiving usual community services.

1f. Emotionally disturbed youth in a community mental health setting with a mental health Axis I externalizing disorder who receive multisystemic therapy will experience decreased severe and disruptive behavior than those receiving usual community services.

1g. Emotionally disturbed youth in a community mental health setting with a mental health Axis I externalizing disorder who receive multisystemic therapy will experience less juvenile justice involvement than those receiving usual community services.

CHAPTER 2

MULTISYSTEMIC THERAPY

2.1 Introduction

Multisystemic Therapy is a well-validated, evidence-based service for the treatment of juvenile offenders (Henggeler, Schoenwald, Borduin, Rowland & Cunningham, 1998; Kazdin & Weiz, 1998; Timmons-Mitchell, Bender, Kishna, Mitchell, 2006). It is a community-based treatment that has achieved favorable long-term outcomes to include reduced out-of-home placement and increased school attendance for children and adolescents presenting with serious clinical problems (Henggeler, 2003). MST was conceived to treat juvenile offenders, yet it has much in common with the system of care movement for the treatment of youth with severe emotional impairment within the communities in which they live (Henggeler, et al., 1998). The purpose of this chapter is to provide an in-depth look at MST. First, the theoretical underpinnings of MST and risk factors associated with youth development of externalizing mental health disorders are discussed. Following is a discussion of MST treatment, MST program design, and MST fidelity measures.

2.2 Theoretical Basis of MST

The theoretical foundation of MST is rooted in systems and social ecological theories (Henggeler et al., 1998). Assessment and treatment within multisystemic therapy are based on social ecological theory (Henggeler et al., 1998). "The treatment

11

theory underlying MST proposes that by addressing the known risk factors and protective factors that directly and indirectly contribute to serious problems in youth (i.e., delinquency, substance abuse, SED), such problems will be reduced" (Schoenwald & Rowland, 2002, p. 95). These problems include physical abuse, neglect, poverty, problems in school, and family dysfunction (Schoenwald & Rowland, 2002). Unlike other evidence-based treatments that focus only on a subset of contributing problems, multisystemic therapy addresses all areas of a youth's environment contributing to problem behavior (Henggeler, Schoenwald, Rowland, & Cunningham, 2002).

2.2.1 Risk Factors Contributing to Serious Problems of Youth

As previously stated, the most problematic disorders of childhood are externalizing disorders such as attention deficit hyperactivity disorder (ADHD), oppositional defiant disorder (ODD), and conduct disorder (CD) due to their high prevalence and association with difficulties in adulthood (Farmer et al., 2002). Left untreated, these externalizing disorders can develop into psychopathological behavior and chronic delinquency (Bergman & Magnusson, 1997; Farmer et al, 2002; Hill, Coie, Lochman, & Greenberg, 2004). Many risk factors contribute to the development of externalizing disorders (Henggeler, Schoenwald et al., 2002; Stormont, 2002). These factors include youth, caregiver, community, and peer group characteristics.

Characteristics of youth correlated with externalizing disorders include negative moods, problems adapting, and inflexibility (Barron & Earls, 1984; as cited in Stormont, 2002). Problem behavior has also been linked to poor social or problem solving skills (Henggeler, Rodick, Borduin, Hanson, Watson, & Urey, 1986). Further,

12

youth who develop externalizing disorders experience difficulty managing their behavior, high reactivity, high irritability, and high intensity (Stormont, 2002). These characteristics can exacerbate problems in relationships between the child and caregivers, peers, and teachers (Henggeler, Schoenwald et al., 2002). Females are underrepresented in the literature on risk factors associated with externalizing disorders; however, trauma exposure appears to be strongly associated with female development of externalizing disorders (Dixon, Howie, & Starling, 2004). Females also have been shown to have higher rates of co-morbidity of externalizing disorders with depressive disorders than males (Anderson, 2002).

Caregiver characteristics that contribute to development of externalizing disorders in children include low levels of social support, high stress, marital conflict, maternal depression, low educational level, substance abuse, and ineffective parenting (Stormont, 2002). In a longitudinal research study (Campbell, 1994), it was found that youth with mothers who were more depressed, more stressed, and more dissatisfied with their marriage were more likely to have pervasive externalizing disorders compared to youth with mothers who were less depressed, less stressed, and more satisfied with their marriage. Other studies support maternal depression (Dumas, Gibson, & Albin, 1989; Fergusson, Lynskey & Horwood, 1993; Nigg & Hinshaw, 1998) or marital discord (Christensen, Phillips, Glasgow, & Johnson, 1983; Emery, 1982) as contributors of youth problem behavior.

Parental psychopathology has also been associated with development of externalizing disorders in children (Faraone, Biederman, Jetton, & Tsuang, 1997;

13

Pfiffner, McBurnett, Lahey, Frick, Loeber, Green, & Rathouz, 1999; Reeves, Werry, Elkind, & Zametkin, 1987). One study examined forms of parental psychopathology to determine if they were related to similar forms of child psychopathology (Pfiffner et al., 1999). An association was found between parental and child externalizing disorders suggesting a familial transmission. This study supports earlier findings of a strong association between paternal externalizing disorders and child externalizing disorders (Faraone et al., 1997; Frick, Lahey, Loeber, Stouthamer-Loeber, Christ, & Hanson, 1992; Lahey, Loeber, Jart, Frick, Applegate, Zhang, Green, & Russo, 1995).

Parenting practices is another area correlated with youth problem behaviors. Parenting styles that are authoritarian or permissive have been linked to youth development of externalizing disorders (Campbell & Ewing, 1990; Henggeler, Schoenwald et al., 2002; Strassberg, Dodge, Bates, & Pettit, 1992). Parents with an authoritarian parenting style are controlling and exhibit a low level of warmth (Henggeler, 2003). Authoritarian parents are highly directive and expect children to follow orders without question. On the other extreme is the permissive style of parenting. Permissive parents have a high level of warmth, but do not provide structure or discipline (Henggeler, 2003). Children with permissive parents are allowed to act in ways that are immature or socially unacceptable. In looking at differences in family variables contributing to externalizing disorders based on gender, the research is mixed. While some research suggests that it takes a worse environment to result in externalizing problems in girls than boys (Lytton & Romney, 1991; Robins, 1991), other research disputes this (Webster-Stratton, 1996).

14

In addition to youth and caregiver characteristics correlated with externalizing disorders; school, community, and peer characteristics have been shown to influence externalizing behaviors. Much research exists on the influence of peer groups on youth behavior (McCallum & Bracken, 1993; Panella & Henggeler, 1986). Transactions with a negative peer group can sustain youth problem behavior (Henggeler et al., 1986; Henggeler, Schoenwald et al., 2002). Communities with high crime, high violence, and lack of opportunity for youth to participate in pro-social activities have also been linked to youth problem behavior (Henggeler, Schoenwald et al., 2002). Rigid school policies, negative teacher-student interactions, and poor academic fit for the youth have further influence on problem behaviors (Henggeler, Schoenwald et al., 2002).

Taking a social ecological approach to assessment and treatment, MST therapists seek to identify all of the risk factors contributing to a youth's emotional and behavioral problems and focus interventions at all identified sources (Henggeler et al., 2002). Interventions might be aimed at the youth, caregivers, school environment, peer group, or many other possible influences on the youth's problems. As the development and sustainability of externalizing disorders comes from many sources, treatment interventions target all of identified problem areas.

2.2.2 Social Ecological Theory

Social ecology goes beyond assessing relations and interactions between the parent and youth. It looks at the effects of all systems in the youth's environment. According to the theory, a developing individual is affected by the environments in which he/she resides as well as by settings in which he or she is not (Bronfenbrenner,

1979). The relationship between people and environments in which they are embedded is dynamic. Each affects the other. The components of ecological systems are the micro-, meso-, exo- and macro-systems (Bronfenbrenner, 1979). It is within the micro-system an individual resides, and it is the micro-system having the most influence on the individual. An example of a micro-system is the family unit of a child. The meso-system includes settings outside the micro-system in which an individual participates (Bronfenbrenner, 1979). The child's school and peer group are examples of meso-systems. Individuals are members of multiple social groups, or meso-systems, at the same time (Earls & Carlson, 2001). As such, MST therapists conduct thorough assessments of the micro- and meso-systems to determine potential contributors to the youths' problems and focus treatment on those areas (Henggeler, Schoenwald et al, 2002). For example, if the assessment determined a mother's depression was contributing to a youth's problems, the MST therapist would focus interventions to treat the mother's depression. At the same time, if the youth were having problems in school, the MST therapist would determine the contributors to the school problems and focus interventions aimed at alleviating the school problems while addressing the mother's depression.

A setting such as the workplace of a child's parent is an exo-system to a child. A child may not come in direct contact with the workplace of a parent; yet, the workplace has an affect on the child, and the child an effect on the workplace. For instance, a parent over-stressed due to pressures of their employment may lack energy to provide a child adequate attention and care. On the other hand, a parent may perform poorly at

16

work due to stress resulting from difficult issues of their child. Thus, MST interventions might be aimed at either helping the parent figure out ways to reduce or manage work stress or aimed at reducing the stress resulting from the youth's difficult issues (Henggeler, Schoenwald et al., 2002).

A governing principle of Social Ecology is the *reciprocation and exchange* (Saleeby, 1992) between the individual and other levels of the ecology. A circular relationship exists in that a change in one area of the system will affect all other levels of the system. Changes in other levels of the system will thus affect the individual (Wakefield, 1996a). Humans will either adapt to their environment or seek to change it (Wakefield, 1996b). An example of reciprocation and exchange can be seen when a child or adolescent is placed in a residential treatment facility to receive mental health treatment aimed at improving problem behaviors. Typically, the child or adolescent fights against the new environment and resists change, yet eventually adapts and problem behaviors improve. If the child or adolescent's family does not make changes in the home environment aimed at sustaining the youth's behavior changes, the problem behaviors eventually return. By providing treatment in the home and community of a youth, MST seeks to make changes across the youth's social ecology that will support sustained improvements of the youth's problems.

Five assumptions underlie the basis for social ecology (Germain & Bloom, 1999). The first assumption is regarding the unit of analysis. A person cannot be studied without including the person's environment in the analysis. Mental health problems develop from multi-layered interactions between the youth and the environment

17

(Henggeler, Schoenwald et al., 2002; Stormont, 2002). To effectively intervene in a youth's mental health problems, assessment must include factors of the youth (biological, genetic, psychological) as well as factors across the entire ecology to understand what sustains or diminishes the problem behavior (Henggeler, Schoenwald et al., 2002). Without this understanding, a practitioner could not be sure of the appropriate interventions to address the problem behavior.

The next assumption is around the person-in-environment fit. This assumption refers to the degree to which one's environment meets a person's needs (Germain & Bloom, 1999). People continuously attempt to adapt to their environment. People either try to improve the fit between themselves and their environment or try to sustain a good fit. A cornerstone of MST is that children's adaptations to chaotic and non-supportive environments may seem pathological (Henggeler, Schoenwald et al., 2002). A goal of MST is to understand the youth's current adaptations and improve the fit between the youth and his or her social ecology in an adaptive fashion, which ties into the third assumption of social ecology. This assumption is that factors exist that either facilitate or impede adaptation. Individuals are usually able to adapt to conventional environments, but may struggle to adapt during stressful times or in conditions where the individual has special needs or limitations (Germain & Bloom, 1999). In the goal of improving the fit between the youth and his or her environment, MST interventions are aimed at removing barriers and developing skills to facilitate positive adaptation (Henggeler, Schoenwald et al., 2002).

18

Flow of life events is assumption number four. As life events occur, people deal with them either positively or negatively, depending on their perception of the event. Negatively perceived events result in the person successfully coping and leading to successful resolution or not being able to cope and leading to an unsuccessful resolution. The response of the individual will affect both the environment and the individual. Successful resolution leads to personal development and/or environmental change. Unsuccessful resolution leads to destruction of the person-environment or maintenance of the status quo. It is the unsuccessful resolution that leads to mental health and problem behavior. Thus, in MST treatment, interventions focus on developing improved coping strategies (Henggeler, Schoenwald et al., 2002).

Finally, the fifth assumption is termed the transacting configuration. This assumption states that in order to understand a life event, one must fully consider all aspects of the person- environment, including all of the systems and subsystems that affect adaptation. These systems and subsystems include a person's cognitive, biological, affective, and behavioral structures in addition to subsystems of the environment. In order to effectively intervene in a youth's problems, a therapist must take into account the dimensions of human temperament and personality in addition to the external environment, culture, and socioeconomic existence of the youth and family (Lazarus, 1996). These five assumptions form the logical basis of social ecology upon which human development can be studied and understood. Again, MST treatment would include a thorough assessment across all these areas and develop interventions

19

aimed at any and all factors contributing to the youth's problems (Henggeler, Schoenwald et al., 2002).

2.2.2.1 Strengths of Social Ecological Theory

The logic of social ecology is one of the strengths of the model in that it takes into account a larger relationship than linear models (Bronfenbrenner, 1979). It allows one to see things in the environment that might either impede or provide an opportunity for a person's growth. Social ecology allows for a fuller assessment of a situation and provides more information than general systems theory, as it encourages the assessment of interactions between systems. Thus, it expands a social worker's thinking as to the cause of problems and allows interventions focused on the total picture, rather than just the individual (Scannapieco & Connell-Carrick, 2005).

Another strength of social ecology is around the use of it as a paradigm, rather than a theory (Greif, 1986). Social workers can use social ecological theory for assessment and then use the treatment methods and techniques they feel best fit the situation. While social ecology as a paradigm is seen as a strength, Wakefield (1996b) considers this strength to also be one of its weaknesses.

2.2.2.2 Weaknesses of Social Ecological Theory

Social ecology does not offer a model of interventions for a problem and is too generic to be relevant to social work practice (Wakefield, 1996b). A fallacy of the logic of social ecology is the focus of interactions between systems. While more than one element may be involved in an interaction, not all of those elements might be a contributor to the problem. Thus, a social worker may conduct a full assessment of the

20

problem, but still target the wrong area for intervention due to lack of understanding of the primary cause of the problem.

Other weaknesses of social ecology include the lack of empirical support and lack of ability to inform about ways in which the person and environment respond to one another or the causal relationship of a problem (Wakefield, 1996b). It does not inform social workers on what or why it is transpiring (Greif, 1986); nor does it allow for prediction of trends and processes (Hudson, 2000).

2.2.2.3 Social Ecological Theory and MST

MST assessment, service provision, and research build off the strengths of social ecology and mitigate the weakness. It builds of the strengths of social ecological theory in that it does not focus just on the individual youth, but provides a clear assessment of the entire ecology and designs interventions aimed at all areas contributing to the youth's problems (Henggeler et al., 1998). It is the role of the MST therapist to assess the factors in the youth's social ecology contributing to identified problems, assess strengths of the social ecology, and develop interventions using the identified strengths to alleviate the problems (Henggeler, et al., 1998). All interactions between systems in the youth's social ecology are investigated from multiple perspectives. Information sources not only include the youth and caregivers; they include teachers, coaches, pastors, grandparents, siblings, or other important figures in the youth's ecology.

Assessment focuses on understanding how various systems contribute to problem behavior, both directly and indirectly (Henggeler, et al., 1998). The therapist takes the information obtained from the various sources and formulates a testable

21

hypothesis as to the causes of the problem behavior. Interventions focus on all aspects of the social ecology contributing to the problems. For example, interventions might focus on problems between caregivers, problems between the youth and school system, or individual problems of a caregiver.

MST therapists work with their MST team, supervisor, and consultant in formulating hypotheses and developing interventions (Henggeler, et al., 1998). The hypotheses are either supported or rejected based on the effectiveness of the interventions. When hypotheses are rejected, the therapist formulates new hypotheses and develops new interventions. Continuous assessment occurs throughout this process. The formulation of testable hypotheses based on a thorough social ecological assessment obtained from many perspectives, along with input from the MST team, supervisor, and consultant, strengthens ecological validity (Henggeler, et al., 1998) and reduces the likelihood of targeting interventions at elements that do not contribute to the problem, a noted weakness of social ecological theory.

2.3 MST Treatment

While the philosophical paradigm of MST is taken from social ecological theory, treatment interventions utilize any number of empirically supported problem-focused treatments, such as cognitive-behavior, family therapies, or parent training (Henggeler, 1999). The goal-oriented treatments focus on well-defined problems based on the needs identified from the social-ecological assessment (Strother, Swenson, & Schoenwald, 1998). "From the perspective of the therapist, treatment is an on-going process of understanding the "fit" between the identified problems and the broader

22

systemic context" (Strother, et al., 1998, p. 6). MST service provision is individually designed based on the needs of the youth and family as identified collaboratively by the family and therapist (Henggeler, et al., 1998). The treatment interventions are developed based on the nine principles of MST (Strother, et al., 1998). (See Appendix A)

MST treatment interventions occur in the youth's natural environment and require the family to actively put forth efforts to reach treatment goals (Henggeler, 1999). Interventions provided in vivo and implemented by the caretakers of the youth further maximize ecological validity and increase the likelihood for treatment generalization and maintenance (Henggeler, et al., 1998). However, it is the responsibility of the therapist and provider agency to ensure treatment goals are being met and families are actively engaged in the treatment process (Strother, et al., 1998). If goals are not being met; the therapist must re-assess the situation, change the treatment strategy, or seek new ways to engage the family (Strother, et al., 1998).

The MST treatment manual spells out the assessment and treatment process for MST (Henggeler, et al., 1998). As discussed in the manual, the MST assessment process is inductive. To help the therapist proceed in a systematic manner, MST Services developed an *Initial Contact Sheet* (Strother, Swenson, & Schoenwald, 1998). The contact sheet guides the therapist to assess all interactions between systems in the youth's social ecology from multiple perspectives. Assessment includes gathering information from many sources in the youth's social ecology. Information sources not only include the youth and parents; they include teachers, coaches, pastors,

23

grandparents, siblings, or other important figures in the youth's ecology (Henggeler, et al., 1998).

Assessment focuses on understanding how various systems contribute to the problem behavior, both directly and indirectly (Henggeler, et al., 1998). The therapist takes the information obtained from the various sources and formulates a testable hypothesis as to the causes of the problem behavior. Interventions focus on all aspects of the social ecology that might be contributing to the problems. "The scope of MST interventions is not limited to the individual adolescent or the family system, but includes difficulties between other systems such as the family-school and family-peer meso-systems" (Henggeler, 1999, p. 3). The strengths of the ecological system identified from the assessment are utilized in the interventions to help mitigate the problems (Henggeler, et al., 1998).

2.4 MST Program Design

The requirements for an agency to become a MST provider are spelled out on the MST website (Multisystemic Therapy Services, 1998a). In order to become a MST provider, an agency must become licensed as a MST provider and agree to adhere to the fidelity of MST. The agency is first evaluated by MST Services for compatibility with the MST treatment model. This evaluation occurs during a site assessment by MST Services staff. All stakeholders of the prospective provider, such as the juvenile probation and agency administrators, participate in the site assessment. "The ideal organizational context is one in which the provider administers a range of family and community-based services that vary in restrictiveness from outpatient, to home-based,

to therapeutic foster care, with even a small short-term residential component"
(Multisystemic Therapy Services, 1998a, p. 2). Once an agency is deemed to be a good
"fit" as a MST provider, the agency becomes licensed and begins the process of
developing MST teams.

MST Services provides guidelines for selecting clinicians who are a good fit for
providing MST (Multisystemic Therapy Services, 1998a). MST therapists are usually
master's level clinicians. A good candidate is one who is highly motivated, flexible,
and possesses a high level of common sense. Each MST clinician maintains a caseload
of four to six families, allowing the clinician time to continuously assess treatment
outcomes and provide an intensive level of treatment to the family in their home and
community (Multisystemic Therapy Services, 1998a). Services are problem-focused
and time-limited, lasting from four to six months (Multisystemic Therapy Services,
1998a). The MST therapist or a member of the therapist's team is available to the
family 24-hours a day, 7-days a week to help the family work through any crisis that
might arise. Unlike most traditional treatments, the MST therapist takes responsibility
for treatment outcomes (Heneggeler, 2003).

MST therapists are supervised by an on-site, highly competent supervisor with
proven clinical skills. The supervisor should have both clinical and administrative
authority over an MST team (Multisystemic Therapy Services, 1998a). Supervisors are
responsible for no more than two teams consisting of two to four therapists each. Prior
to providing or supervising MST; each therapist, supervisor, and administrator of the
provider organization receives a 5-day training on MST principles, theoretical

underpinnings, cultural competency, treatment strategies, and service provision (Multisystemic Therapy Services, 1998a). Once service provision begins, the on-site supervisor provides regularly scheduled, weekly, clinical supervision to the MST team and monitors the therapists' adherence to MST fidelity (Multisystemic Therapy Services, 1998a). "Like MST interventions, supervision is pragmatic and goal-oriented. Therapists are expected to conceptualize cases in multisystemic terms, and supervision is directed toward articulating treatment priorities, obstacles to success, and designing interventions to successfully navigate those obstacles" (Multisystemic Therapy Services, 1998a, p. 3).

In addition to on-site supervision, each MST team and supervisor works closely with an assigned consultant from MST Services who monitors therapist and supervisor adherence to MST fidelity, helps set up on-site clinical supervision that facilitates fidelity adherence, helps the team overcome treatment barriers, and helps develop treatment strategies (Strother, et al., 1998). Each week, the MST team sends required MST paperwork to the consultant and then participates in consultation via phone conferencing. In addition, the consultant provides a quarterly, on-site, booster training for the supervisor and therapists (Strother, et al., 1998). If systems barriers have been identified that interfere with successful treatment and/or therapist adherence to MST fidelity, the consultant works with the team, supervisor, administrator, and stakeholders to identify ways to remove the barriers (Strother, et al., 1998).

2.5 MST Treatment Fidelity

Adherence to MST treatment fidelity is determined by measuring therapist and supervisor adherence to the nine principles of MST (Huey, Henggeler, Rowland, Halliday-Boykins, Cunningham, & Pickrel, 2004). A higher level of fidelity to the MST model has been correlated to stronger outcomes than poorer adherence to the model (Henggeler, Melton, Brondino, Scherer, & Henley, 1997; Henggeler, Pickerel, & Brondino, 1999; Schoenwald, Henggeler, Brondino, & Rowland, 2000). Therapist adherence to the nine principles is measured by the Therapist Adherence Measure (TAM) (Henggeler & Borduin, 1992). The TAM is a standardized, 26-item likert scale developed through expert consensus and validated in two MST trials (Henggeler et al., 1997; Henggeler, Pickerel et al., 1999). The TAM is administered by someone other than the therapist to the youth and family each month they are receiving treatment (Henggeler & Borduin, 1992). The TAM scores are aggregated for each therapist to guide clinical supervision and consultation (Henggeler & Borduin, 1992). To ensure supervisors provide clinical supervision according to the MST principles, MST therapists complete a Supervisor Adherence Measure (SAM) (Henggeler & Borduin, 1992) every other month on their supervisor. The scores from the SAMs are aggregated for use by the consultant and program administrator in supervision with the MST supervisor (Henggeler & Borduin, 1992).

CHAPTER 3

EMPIRICAL RESEARCH REVIEW OF MST

3.1 Introduction

This chapter will provide an overview of the empirical literature on MST. Included in the overview of MST research are study designs, study samples, operationalization of independent and dependent variables, and data analysis. A critical review of the literature is provided, followed by findings of MST research.

3.2 Method

A research review was conducted to locate peer-reviewed research studies examining the effectiveness of MST with youth who have serious clinical problems. The research review was conducted using the key words Multisystemic therapy, MST, Multisystemic treatment and was crossed referenced with the keywords outcome studies, treatment outcomes, and empirical studies. Databases searched included PsychINFO, Academic Search Premier, Social Work Abstracts, and Social Services Abstracts. In addition, a thorough search of related peer reviewed journals was conducted.

Several studies were found examining the effectiveness of MST. In addition, several follow-up studies addressing the long-term effectiveness of MST, as well as studies reporting on therapist adherence to fidelity of the MST model were located. Finally, information on current studies in progress and studies that have been completed but not peer-reviewed were found. The studies found were narrowed down to peer-reviewed, randomized, controlled studies of MST and any follow-up studies of the randomized studies. Of particular interest were studies that reported on outcomes of family relations, interactions or functioning; out-of-home placement; psychiatric symptoms; and school functioning or attendance. These outcomes were of particular interest for this paper as they are important outcome areas for improving the lives of children and adolescents with an emotional disturbance (Zaff et al., 2002).

3.3 Results of Empirical Research Search

Of the research articles initially reviewed, 18 studies were chosen for inclusion in this paper based on the methods described previously, six of which were follow-up studies (see Table 3.1). Seven studies were randomized trials with juvenile offenders identified as chronic and/or violent (Borduin, Henggeler, Blaske, & Stein, 1990; Borduin, Mann, Cone, Henggeler, Fucci, Blaski, & Williams, 1995; Henggeler, Roddic, Borduin, Hanson, Watson, & Urey, 1986; Henggeler, Melton, Smith, 1992; Henggeler, Melton, Brondino, Scherer, & Hanley, 1997; Scherer, & Brondino, 1994; Timmons-Mitchell, Bender, Kishna, & Mitchell, 2006), one of which focused on inner-city juvenile offenders (Henggeler, et al., 1986). These studies compared MST to individual counseling (Borduin et al., 1990; Borduin et al., 1995) or usual community services (Henggeler et al., 1986; Henggeler et al., 1992; Henggler, Melton et al., 1997; Scherer, & Brondino, 1994; Timmons-Mitchell et al. 2006).

An eighth study (Brunk, Henggeler, & Whelen, 1987) compared MST against parent behavioral training by randomly assigning maltreating families to either a MST group or a control group. One study compared MST with usual community services for delinquent youth identified as substance abusing or dependent (Henggeler, Pickrel, & Brondino, 1999). The purpose of another study (Henggeler, Halliday-Boykins, Cunningham, Randall, Shapiro, & Chapman, 2006) was to compare a drug court model with family court model rather than to specifically measure MST outcomes. Since MST outcomes were included in the study, the results are included in this review.

Table 3.1   Randomized Clinical Studies of MST

Author(s)	Population	Sample Size	Comparison	Study Type	Statistics Used	Findings
Henggeler, Roddic, Borduin, Hanson, Watson, & Urey, 1986	Inner city Juvenile offenders 10-17 77% male 56% Black 42% White 2% Hispanic	33 Exp 23 Con	Usual community services	Pre-Post Randomized clinical trial	MANCOVA ANOVA for any significant measure found	Improved family relations Decreased behavior problems
Brunk, Henggeler, & Whelan, 1987	Maltreating Families 55% male 43% African American 57% White	16 Exp 17 Con	Behavior Parent Training	Pre-Post Randomized clinical trial	t-test to compare completers vs non-completers ANOVA & Chi-square to compare groups pre-test MANCOVA with child and parental age as covariates ANOVA for pre-post effects	Improved parent-child interactions
Borduin, Henggeler, Blaske, & Stein, 1990	Juvenile Sex Offenders 81.9% male 80.6 Black 19.4 White	8 Exp 8 Con	Individual Counseling	Pre-post Randomized Clinical trial	Between group comparison of re-arrests using Fisher's Exact Test	Reduced recidivism of sexual offending
Henggeler, Melton & Smith, 1992	Violent and chronic Juvenile offenders ME 15.2 77% male 56% Black 42% White 2% Hispanic	43 Exp 41 Con	Usual Community Services	Pre-Post Randomized clinical trial	ANOVA & Chi-square to compare completers vs. non-completers ANOVA to compare groups at pre-test and post-test	Improved family relations Improved peer relations Decreased out-of-home placements
Henggeler, Melton, Smith Schoenwald, & Hanley, 1993	Follow-up study to 1992 Same as previous	Same as previous	Same as previous	2.4 year follow-up for arrests	Survival Analysis	More effective in preventing future criminal behavior

30

Table 3.1 continued

Author(s)	Population	Sample Size	Comparison	Study Type	Statistics Used	Findings
Scherer & Brondino, 1994	Violent juvenile offenders at risk of incarceration ME 15.12 yo 81% Male 78% African American 22% White	23 Exp 21 Con	Usual Probation Services	Pre-Post Randomized clinical trial	ANOVA to compare groups at post-test No comparison of groups pre-test mentioned	Decreased aggression Improved conduct Improved parental monitoring Non-significant results on attention problems, anxiety, & psychosis
Borduin, Mann, Cone, Henggeler, Fucci, Blaski & Williams, 1995	Violent and chronic juvenile offenders ME 14.8 yo 67.5% Male 30% 70% White	76 Exp 56 Con	Individual Counseling	Pre-Post Randomized clinical trial	ANOVA & Chi-square to compare completers vs. non-completers and to compare groups at pre-test MANOVA to test tx outcomes	Improved family relations, Decreased MH symptoms, 4-year f/u decreased criminal behavior
Schaeffer & Borduin, 2005	f/u to Borduin et al. (1995) Same as above ME at f/u = 28.9 yo	92 Exp 84 Con Inclusion of tx non-comp.	Individual Counseling	Binary Logistic Regression Survival Analysis	Binary Logistic Regression to describe risk of arrest between groups Survival Analysis to determine proportion who survived any re-arrest Effect Size	MST group less likely to be rearrested and less likely to be rearrested for violent offenses, non-violent, and drug offenses
Henggeler, Melton, Brondino, Scherer & Hanley, 1997	Violent and chronic juvenile offenders ME 15.22 81.9% Male 80.6% African Amer 19.4% White	87 Exp 73 Con	Usual community services	Pre-Post Randomized clinical trial	ANOVA & Chi-square to compare completers vs. non-completers and to compare groups at pre-test ANOVA to test tx outcomes t-test when significance found	Decreased psychiatric symptoms, decreased days in out-of-home placement 1.7 year follow-up – rate of re-arrest did not drop significantly (attributed to low fidelity to MST)
Henggeler, Rowland, Randall, Ward, Pickerel, Cunningham Miller, Hand, Zealberg, Edwards, & Santos, 1999	Youth presenting psychiatric services ME 12.9 65% Male 64% African American 34% White 1% Asian 1% Hispanic	56 Exp 54 Control	Inpatient psychiatric unit with behavioral milieu, followed by usual community services	Mixed factorial random assignment	ANOVA & Chi-square to compare completers vs. non-completers and to compare groups at pre-test ANOVA to test tx outcomes t-test when significance found	Decreased externalizing problems, improved family relations, improved school attendance

Table 3.1 continued

Author(s)	Population	Sample Size	Comparison	Study Type	Statistics Used	Findings
Henggeler, Rowland, Halliday-Boykins, Sheidow, Ward, Randall, Pickerel, Cunningham & Edwards, 2003	Youth from 1999 study (1 year follow-up) above.	Same as 1999	Same as 1999	Mixed effects growth curve modeling	Mixed-effects Growth Modeling to allow evaluation of linear & non-linear change over time. To measure symptoms, out of home placement, & family functioning	Both groups converged in all areas by 1 year. No long lasting effects of tx
Huey, Henggeler, Rowland, Halliday-Boykins, Cunningham, Pickrel, & Edwards, 2004	Youth from 1999 study presenting with suicidal ideation, plan or attempt ME 12.9	Same as 1999 study	Same as 1999 study	Mixed effects growth curve modeling	Mixed-effects Growth Modeling General Linear Mixed Model	Decreased rates of suicide attempts at 1 year follow-up, reduced psychiatric symptom
Henggeler, Pickrel, & Brondino, 1999	Juvenile offenders with co-occurring psychiatric diagnosis ME 15.7 50% Black 47% White 3% Other	58 Exp 60 Con	Usual community services	Pre-Post Randomized clinical trial	ANOVA & Chi-square to compare groups at pre-test. ANOVA to test tx outcomes	High level of treatment completion, increased mainstream school attendance, cost savings, decreased criminal activities, decreased substance abuse
Brown, Henggeler, Schoenwald, Brondino & Pickrel, 1999	6-month follow-up to 1999 study 79% Male	Same as above	Same as above	Multimethod (self-report, parent report, archival) strategies to study school attendance	One-way Analysis of Variance (ANOVA) to compare groups pre-test ANOVA at 6-mos post-tx to compare groups	Increased school involvement, sustained school attendance over time through 6-month follow-up
Henggeler, Clingempeel, Brondino & Pickrel, 2002	4 year follow-up to 1999 study 76% Male 60% African American 40% White	Same as above	Same as above	Multi-method (self-report, biological, and archival measures) assessment battery to measure criminal behavior, illicit drug use and psychiatric symptoms	ANOVA & Chi-square to compare tx groups of research continuers and to compare attrition for f/u study. MANCOVA with marijuana use and youth age held as covariates due to difference noted on baseline comparison One – way ANCOVA for significant measures from MANCOVA	No long-term effects for psychiatric symptoms, decreased aggressive crimes, no significant difference in number of property crimes, mixed effects in long-term drug use

32

Table 3.1 continued

Author(s)	Population	Sample Size	Comparison	Study Type	Statistics Used	Findings
Rowland, Halliday-Boykins, Henggeler, Cunningham Lee, Kruesi, & Shapiro, 2005	9 to 17 year old youth with a severe emotional disturbance at imminent risk of out-of-home placement. ME 14.5 58% male, 42 % female 84% multiracial 10% Caucasian 7% Asian American & Pacific Islander	15 Exp. 16 Con	Usual Services	Pre-Post with control Randomized clinical trial	ANOVA & Chi-square to compare groups at pre-test 1-way ANCOVA with self-reported delinquency held as a covariate to measure between group differences for archival measures To compensate for analysis being underpowered, Cohen's D to measure effect size	Reduction in externalizing, internalizing, and minor criminal activity. Fewer days in out-of-home placement. Increased social support for caretakers. No difference in substance use No treatment effects for family functioning
Henggeler, Halliday-Boykins, Cunningham Randall, Shapiro, & Chapman, 2006	Juvenile drug offenders ME 15..2 yo 83% male 17% female 67% African American 31% White 2% Biracial	42 FCt/US 38 DC/US 38 D/MST 43 D/MST/CM	FCt/US DCt/US DCt/MST DCt/MST/CM	4 condition randomized control study Purpose to compare Family Court with Drug Court	ANOVA & Chi-square to compare tx groups at pre-tx. 4x3 doubly multivariate (RMANOVA) ANOVA for sign. results Cohen's D to measure effect size	Drug Ct more effective than Family Ct. No significant findings for MST or MST/CM over drug court with usual services
Timmons-Mitchell, Bender, Kishna, & Mitchell, 2006	Juvenile Offenders ME 15.1 yo 88% male 22% female 15.5% African American 77.5% White 4.2% Hispanic 2.8% bi-racial	48 MST 45 US	Usual Treatment	Randomized controlled study with 18 month f/u for offense data, 6-month f/u for youth functioning and symptoms	Likelihood and relative odds ratio for re-arrest Survival analysis Linear modeling	Reduction in re-arrest Improvement in functioning Improvement in mood and emotion No significant changes in substance use

As previously discussed, only two studies exist on the use of MST with non-juveniles with a severe emotional disturbance (Henggeler, Rowland, Randall, Ward, Pickrel, Cunningham et al., 1999; Rowland et al., 2005). One of the studies compared a modified version of MST as an alternative to psychiatric hospitalization for youth who are suicidal or in acute psychiatric distress (Henggeler et al., 1999). Results of this study were favorable with MST outcomes. The second study, which compared MST with

33

usual services for youth with a severe emotional disturbance, also found favorable MST outcomes (Rowland et al., 2005).

Sample sizes of the studies noted in Table 1 ranged from 16 to 155. The majority of the participants were male, with a strong mix of ethnic diversity. Ages of youth ranged from 9 to 17. Of the MST studies reporting on family composition, 3 percent to 31 percent lived with both biological and/or adoptive parents. The majority of the youth lived with at least one biological parent, most often the mother. The average children in the home ranged from 2.7 to 3.1. The average age of caregivers ranged from 10.5 years to 12 years of education and nearly all were reported to be from lower socio-economic status.

3.3.1 Characteristics of MST

Therapists providing MST across all studies were either master's level therapists or attending graduate school. They included a mix of both males and females and of diverse ethnic groups. Caseload sizes ranged from three to six families. MST services were provided in the homes and communities of participants and lasted an average of four to six months. All the studies reported the MST therapists received an average of 40 hours of training in multisystemic treatment prior to provision, plus received weekly consultation, supervision, and quarterly booster sessions with a MST consultant. It should be noted one of the founders of MST provided the consultation/supervision in all but one of the studies (Timmons-Mitchell et al., 2006).

3.3.2 Characteristics of Comparison Groups

Seven studies compared MST with *usual community services* (Henggeler et al., 1986; Henggeler et al., 1992; Henggeler et al., 1997; Henggeler et al., 1999; Rowland et al., 2005, Scherer & Brondino, 1994; Timmons-Mitchell et al., 2006). Usual community services varied greatly among the studies. In four of the studies, usual services were clinic-based and in combination with traditional probation (Henggeler et al., 1986; Henggeler et al., 1992; Henggeler et al., 1997; Henggeler et al., 1999). One study compared MST with Hawaii's existing continuum of care services, which included a range of services, including in-home, outpatient, and out-of-home placements (Rowland et al., 2005).

Three studies compared MST with individual counseling (Borduin et al., 1990; Borduin et al, 1995; Schaeffer & Borduin, 2005). Parental behavior training was the comparison treatment in one study (Brunk et al., 1987). Parental behavior training included weekly group sessions in a clinic-based setting provided at a ratio of one therapist to seven participants. The group sessions focused on teaching parents positive reinforcement, parental consistency, and disciplinary techniques.

In the study comparing MST to psychiatric hospitalization (Henggeler et al., 1999), youth in the comparison group received acute stabilization from a multi-disciplinary treatment team. The team included a child and adolescent psychiatrist, a master's level social worker, a teacher trained in special education and nursing staff. Upon discharge from the hospital, youth were linked with mental health providers in the community for follow-up care. Finally, in the study designed to compare drug court

35

with family court (Henggeler et al., 2006) youth referred to juvenile services for a drug related offense were randomly assigned to one of four conditions. Youth were either assigned to family court with usual services, drug court with usual services, drug court with MST, or drug court with an enhanced MST model.

3.3.3 Operationalization of Dependent Variables

Many measurement tools were used across studies to measure treatment outcomes. As the original intent of MST was to treat juvenile offenders and reduce offending behavior (Henggeler et al., 1998), one would expect to find re-arrest being measured in the majority of MST studies, as was the case. Eight of the 12 randomized studies (Borduin et al., 1990; Henggeler et al., 1992; Henggeler et al., 1997; Henggeler et al, 1999; Henggeler, Pickrel et al., 1999; Rowland, et al, 2005; Henggeler et al., 2006; and Timmons-Mitchell et al., 2006), as well as 3 follow-up studies (Henggeler et al, 1993; Schaeffer & Borduin, 2005; Henggeler, Clingempeel et al., 2002) measured re-arrest using archived criminal records. In addition, four studies used the Self-Report Delinquency Scale (SRDS) along with archived criminal records to measure offending behavior and re-arrest (Henggeler et al., 1997; Henggeler et al., 2006; Rowland et al, 2005; Henggeler, Clingempeel et al., 2002). An additional study (Scherer & Brondino, 1994) used the SRDS as the only measurement of criminal offending.

As previously mentioned, of particular interest were studies reporting on outcomes affecting youth psychiatric symptoms; family functioning; out-of-home placement; and school functioning as these are important outcome areas for improving lives of children and adolescents with an emotional disturbance (Zaff et al., 2002). All but one of the randomized studies (Borduin et al., 1990) reported on youth psychiatric symptoms. The Child Behavior Checklist (CBCL) was used in all studies reporting on mental health symptoms except one (Timmons-Mitchell et al., 2006), which used the Child and Adolescent Functional Assessment Scale (CAFAS). In addition to the CBCL, some studies added the Brief Symptom Inventory (Henggeler et al., 1997; Henggeler et al., 1999; Henggeler et al., 2003; Huey et al., 2004; Scherer & Brondino, 1994) or the Symptom Checklist – Revised 90 (Brunk et al., 1987; Henggeler et al., 1992; Borduin et al., 1995) as a secondary measure of youth symptomology and behaviors.

Family functioning was measured in the majority of the studies. The most common measure of family functioning noted across studies was the Family Adaptability and Cohesion Evaluation Scale (FACES - III), which was used in six studies (Borduin et al., 1995; Henggeler et al., 1992; Henggeler et al., 1997; Henggeler et al., 1998; Henggeler et al., 2003; Rowland et al., 2005). Other measures of family functioning used in MST trials included the Eysenck Personal Inventory (Henggeler et al., 1986), the Family Inventory on Life Events and Changes (Brunk et al., 1987), and the Family Assessment Measure III (Scherer & Brondino, 1994).

Few studies measured out-of-home placement or school functioning. Out-of-home placement was measured in two studies through archived records and family self-report (Henggeler et al., 1999; Rowland et al., 2005). School functioning was measured in four studies through archived records (Rowland et al., 2005; Brown et al., 1999), the Service Utilization Survey (Henggeler et al., 1999; Henggeler et al., 2003; Brown et al., 1999), and/or the Self-Report Delinquency Scale (Rowland et al., 2005).

37

3.3.4 Data Analysis of Studies

With the exception of one randomized controlled study (Timmons-Mitchell et al., 2006), analysis of variance (ANOVA) or multiple analysis of covariance (MANCOVA) was used to determine change from pre-test to post-test. Demographic characteristics and pre-test scores between experimental and control groups were compared to ensure equivalency of groups using chi-square and ANOVA in the later MST studies (Borduin et al, 1995; Brunk et al., 1987; Henggeler, et al., 1992; Henggeler, et al., 1997; Henggeler, et al., 1999; Henggeler, et al., 2006; Rowland, et al., 2005, Schaeffer & Borduin, 2005; Timmons-Mitchell, et al., 2006). When differences were noted between groups, multivariate analysis of covariance (MANCOVA) or analysis of co-variance (ANCOVA), holding the group differences as covariates to control for such differences was used.

One follow-up study (Brown et al., 1999) used ANOVA to compare groups at 6-months post treatment, while another follow-up study used ANOVA to compare groups at 4-years post treatment (Henggeler et al., 2002). Other follow-up studies used mixed-effects growth modeling to evaluate linear and non-linear change over time (Henggeler et al., 2003; Huey et al., 2004), survival analysis to determine the proportion of participants in each group not experiencing re-arrest (Henggeler et al., 1993; Schaeffer & Borduin, 1994), and/or binary logistic regression to describe the risk of arrest between groups (Schaeffer & Borduin, 1994).

38

3.4 Critique of Methods

The 12 clinical trials included random assignment to either the experimental group or a control group and pre/post-testing (Borduin et al., 1990; Borduin et al, 1995; Brunk et al., 1987; Henggeler et al., 1986; Henggeler et al., 1992; Henggeler et al., 1997; Henggeler et al., 1999; Henggeler et al., 2006; Rowland et al., 2005; Schaeffer & Borduin, 2005; Scherer & Brondino, 1994; Timmons-Mitchell et al., 2006), thus controlling for most threats to internal validity (Rubin & Babbie, 2005). Differential attrition was a threat to internal validity of some studies (Borduin et al., 1990; Borduin et al., 1995; Brunk et al., 1987; Henggeler et al., 1986; Henggeler et al., 1992; Henggeler et al., 1997). The majority of studies noted statistical control of attrition (Borduin et al., 1995; Brunk et al., 1987; Henggeler et al., 1997), but some did not (Borduin et al., 1990; Henggeler et al., 1986; Henggeler et al., 1992). While measuring fidelity to MST is mandatory for all MST providers, not all of the studies, particularly the earlier studies, reported fidelity outcomes (e.g.: Henggeler et al., 1986; Brunk et al., 1987; Borduin et al., 1990). While one might assume MST fidelity was adhered to, this can not be ascertained, thus threatening study internal validity compromising study findings.

The use of chi-square and analysis of variance (ANOVA) in the later MST studies to ensure equivalency of groups was a strength in those studies, allowing researchers to control for between-group differences when differences were found using MANCOVA or ANCOVA. Both ANCOVA and MANCOVA test for differences between the treatment group and comparison group after adjusting for differences

39

among covariates (Tabachnick & Fidell, 2001). Using MANCOVA provides a clearer picture of the effects of independent variables on multiple dependent variables and a more sensitive statistical test that reduces unwanted error and improves the chances of rejecting a false null hypothesis (Tabachnick & Fidell, 2001). Three of the earliest studies (Henggeler et al., 1986; Borduin et al., 1990; Scherer & Brondino, 1994) and one later study (Timmons-Mitchell et al., 2006) did not mention statistical comparison of groups pre-test. However, random assignment of subjects to treatment groups enhanced the likelihood groups were comparable (Rosenthal, 2001).

Mixed-effects growth modeling used in follow-up studies (Henggeler et al., 2003; Huey et al., 2004) was appropriate for evaluating linear and non-linear change over time, as it is a powerful tool for repeated measures of grouped data which is balanced or unbalanced (Tabachnick & Fidell, 2001). Due to the classic experimental design of the studies and the researcher's control of demographic characteristics, pre-test scores, and control for attrition in the majority of studies; the studies appear to possess strong internal validity. However, further strengths and limitations should be noted across studies.

One study had only eight subjects in each treatment group (Borduin et al., 1990). Of the 16 total subjects, 6 did not complete treatment, but were included in the study. The researchers chose to include the 6 non-completers because they felt they received enough treatment (at least 4 months) to be included. The study finding reported by the researchers was youth receiving MST had reduced re-arrests compared to youth receiving individual therapy. The offenses committed by youth in this study were sexual

40

offenses ranging from exhibitionism to rape. No analysis was conducted to determine if type of sexual offense might be a confounding variable in the rate of re-arrest. The study also fails to mention any comparison of the groups pre-test. Due to the small sample size, high number of treatment non-completers, lack of comparison between the groups, and lack of control for confounding variables, this study has serious limitations.

As mentioned, all of the randomized studies and follow-up studies published to date, with the exception of one (Timmons-Mitchell et al., 2006), have been conducted by one of the founders of MST. As such, Littell, Popa, & Forsythe (2005), through the Cochrane Collaboration, conducted a meta-analysis of MST studies to evaluate its efficacy. The authors found inconclusive evidence of MST effectiveness when compared to other interventions. They noted their small study size, lack of evidence for other interventions more effective than MST, and comprehensiveness of the treatment suggest support for more independent studies of MST.

A prior meta-analysis of MST was conducted by Curtis, Ronan, & Borduin (2004). They reported favorable MST outcomes. As noted by Littell et al. (2005), their findings may have been affected by estimation errors and bias due to the fact the researchers were program developers of MST. There also exists controversy over meta-analysis. According to Nugent (2006), two conditions must be met in order for a meta-analysis to be valid. True scores of measures must be linear; and, there must exist between the measures magnitude of the error variances a special linear relationship. Otherwise, the error variances are random or spurious. The Littell et al. (2005) meta-analysis included studies not published in peer reviewed journals and included

41

comparison of variables measured differently across the studies; therefore, it is questionable as to whether the meta-analysis met the conditions discussed by Nugent (2006).

Many of the measurement tools used across studies have been shown to be reliable and valid instruments. While most of the studies include brief statements as to the validity of the instruments used, a few of the studies do not (Brunk et al, 1987; Henggeler et al, 1992). One of the strengths across studies is the consistent use of the same measurement tools to measure youth symptomology and family functioning, allowing future comparison across studies. Another strength of measurement of dependent variables is use of many sources to measure the same construct. The method of using different methods to collect the same information, triangulation, reduces the likelihood of measurement error (Rubin & Babbie, 2004). Many of the MST studies used triangulation for measuring dependent variables by using more than one measurement tool and obtaining information from multiple sources such as the youth, parent(s), and teacher(s) (Henggeler et al., 1997; Henggeler et al., 1999; Henggeler et al., 2003; Huey et al., 2004; Scherer & Brondino, 1994).

As can be seen, MST has been compared to a multitude of other treatments. Most of the studies reported on the effectiveness of MST in reducing criminal behavior, improving family relationships, and though not always sustained, improving psychiatric symptoms. Despite the mentioned limitations to MST studies, the overwhelming results support further study of MST for treating youth with serious mental health disorders and have implications for social work practice, policy, and research.

42

<u>3.5 Findings of MST Studies</u>

Most of the studies reported on the effectiveness of MST in improving family relationships and/or decreasing offending behavior. Improved peer relationships were reported in one of the studies (Henggeler et al., 1992); and three studies reported improved school attendance and/or performance (Henggeler, Rowland et al., 1999; Henggeler, Pickrel et al., 1999; Brown et al., 1999). Decreased behavior problems and/or improved psychiatric symptoms were present in five of the studies (Henggeler et al., 1986; Borduin et al., 1995; Henggeler et al., 1997; Henggeler, Rowland et al., 1999; Huey et al., 2004). One area of disappointment was the results of the 4-year follow-up (Henggeler, Clingempeel et al., 2002) to the study of youth with co-occurring substance abuse and psychiatric diagnosis (Henggeler, Pickrel et al., 1999). No long-term effects of improved psychiatric symptoms existed. It is important to note the study did not address if any of the participants were receiving any type of on-going psychiatric treatment, such as medication management. Further, many of the participants (as many as 50%) were reported to still be using cocaine or marijuana at the time of the follow-up, which could interfere with mental health functioning. The researchers did not correlate on-going psychiatric symptoms with substance use, so it is not known if the participants still using drugs were the same participants reported as having on-going psychiatric symptoms. The researchers also identified a weakness in the original study finding a low level of MST therapists' adherence to treatment fidelity. It is not known what effects, if any, this might have on the outcomes of the on-going psychiatric symptoms.

43

In the study comparing MST to psychiatric hospitalization (Henggler, Rowland et al., 1999), 44% of the youth in the treatment group required emergency psychiatric hospitalization during the treatment phase of the study to maintain the safety of the participants. In order to control for the effects of hospitalization, youth in the MST group were kept separate from the rest of the hospital milieu, and the MST treatment team remained responsible for the treatment of the youth while in the hospital. However, regardless of attempts to control for the overlapping of services, the outcomes of this study are seriously limited (Henggeler, Rowland et al., 1999).

Suicidality was compared between the MST group and the control group (Huey et al., 2004) and the researchers noted the experimental group, though randomly assigned, had higher rates at pre-test of suicidal ideation, depressive affect, and feelings of hopelessness. Therefore, the significant decrease in suicide attempts at 1-year follow-up may have been *regression to the mean* (Rubin and Babbie, 2004) rather than improvements due to the treatment. The researchers report a lack of external validity due to the fact youth who attempt suicide are a heterogeneous group and due to the study sample being composed mostly of African American youth. According to the researchers, African American youth attempt suicide at lower rates than other youth, which further reduces the external validity of the study.

While MST was found to have significant improvement across many areas in all the studies, instances were found where usual services were as effective as MST for certain variables. In the study by Brunk et al. (1987), both MST and usual services groups experienced a significant level of improvement in youth mental health

44

symptoms/problem behavior and in family problems. However, the MST group experienced significant improvement in positive family interactions compared to the usual services group.

A follow-up study (Henggeler, Clingempeel et al., 2002) found that while the MST group initially experienced improvement in psychiatric symptoms, the effects were not maintained 4-years post treatment. The study also failed to find a significant difference in the number of property crimes between the MST group and the comparison group and the effects for drug use were mixed. Another study (Rowland et al., 2005) found that neither MST nor the comparison group experienced statistically significant improvement in substance use or family functioning.

The only randomized study published to date by researchers not affiliated with the founders of MST (Timmons-Mitchell et al., 2006) found significant improvements for MST compared with usual treatment in the areas of youth functioning and mental health symptoms. While they did find a significant difference between treatment groups for re-arrests, the results were not as significant as found in previous MST trials. They also did not find a significant improvement in substance use, but noted a small number of youth in the sample that used drugs or alcohol.

CHAPTER 4

METHODS

4.1 Introduction

This chapter includes an overview of the research study design and the research hypotheses to be answered. The study population, study sample, and data collection methods are discussed. The operationalization of the independent and dependent variables of the study are delineated. Finally, the data analysis process is discussed.

4.2 Research Design

This study compared multisystemic therapy to *usual services* in a community mental health setting for emotionally disturbed youth with externalizing disorders. Usual services included the combination of intensive case management with a family skills training curriculum. A secondary data analysis utilizing a pretest-post-test, quasi-experimental design was used. The design was a quasi-experimental design, as it lacked random assignment. It was modeled after a design called *overflow design* (Rubin & Babbie, 2008), which was deemed a non-equivalent comparison group design. As with the design discussed in Rubin and Babbie (2008), youth meeting criteria for study inclusion based on diagnostic criteria (those with an externalizing disorder), no juvenile justice involvement, and scores on a standardized measurement tool (CEA-RDM) were assigned a treatment condition based on whether a slot existed on a MST caseload at the time of assignment and whether the family agreed to services. "Despite lacking random

46

assignment, this design would probably possess adequate internal validity, because it seemed unlikely that families that happened to be referred when caseloads are full would not be comparable to families that happen to be referred when caseloads are not full" (Rubin and Babbie, 2004, p. 353). This study tested the following research hypotheses.

4.3 Research Hypotheses

4.3.1 Overarching Hypothesis

Emotionally disturbed youth in a community mental health setting with an externalizing disorder who receive multisystemic therapy will experience more improved treatment outcomes than those receiving usual community services.

4.3.2 Secondary Hypotheses

1a. Emotionally disturbed youth in a community mental health setting with an externalizing disorder who receive multisystemic therapy will experience more improved mental health symptoms than those receiving usual community services.

1b. Emotionally disturbed youth in a community mental health setting with an externalizing disorder who receive multisystemic therapy will experience more improved functioning than those receiving usual community services.

1c. Emotionally disturbed youth in a community mental health setting with an externalizing disorder who receive multisystemic therapy will experience more improved school behavior than those receiving usual community services.

47

1d. Emotionally disturbed youth in a community mental health setting with an externalizing disorder who receive multisystemic therapy will experience more improved family functioning than those receiving usual community services.

1e. Emotionally disturbed youth in a community mental health setting with an externalizing disorder who receive multisystemic therapy will experience decreased risk of self harm than those receiving usual community services.

1f. Emotionally disturbed youth in a community mental health setting with an externalizing disorder who receive multisystemic therapy will experience decreased severe and aggressive behavior than those receiving usual community services.

1g. Emotionally disturbed youth in a community mental health setting with a mental health Axis I externalizing disorder who receive multisystemic therapy will experience less juvenile justice involvement than those receiving usual community services.

4.4 Study Population

Youth included in this project were those identified as having an emotional disturbance with a DSM-IV (American Psychiatric Association, 1994) mental health externalizing disorder (i.e.: ADHD, conduct disorder, oppositional defiant disorder). Youth were under the age of 18 and had not been adjudicated or awaiting possible adjudication with juvenile court. Further, the youth had to have at least one legally authorized representative (LAR) willing to participate in treatment and met the Texas Department of Mental Health Mental Retardation Child and Adolescent Texas

48

Recommended Authorization guidelines for intensive in-home treatment, service package 2.2 (Texas Department of Mental Health Mental Retardation, 2004). Eligibility for service package 2.2 is determined by the existence of an externalizing disorder, a score of 18 or over on the Ohio Youth Problem Severity Scale, a score of 50 or less on the Ohio Youth Functioning Scale, plus a score of 4 or 5 on Severe Disruptive Aggressive Behaviors, or a score of 4 or 5 on Family Resources, or a score of 5 on History of Treatment, or a score of 4 or 5 in School Behavior.

4.4.1 Community Mental Health Services Eligibility

Entrance into MHMR of Tarrant County child and adolescent services (a community mental health center under the auspices of TDMHMR, now the Department of State Health Services), requires the legally authorized representative of a youth experiencing possible mental health symptoms call the MHMR Screening and Crisis line. Youth are often referred to the community mental health center from the school and juvenile justice systems. Youth are mostly referred from these systems due to disruptive, acting out, and or aggressive behaviors. However, though these systems may refer the youth, the youth's legal guardian must be the one to call the screening and crisis line and agree for the youth to participate in treatment. During the initial call to the screening and crisis line, a Qualified Mental Health Professional (a bachelor's level person with a human services degree) completes a brief screening to determine potential eligibility for MHMR services. Eligible youth include those with a DSM-IV mental health diagnoses on Axis I (American Psychiatric Association, 1994) in addition to being at-risk of placement, or, are identified by the school system as *emotionally disturbed*, or, who have a severe functional impairment due to the symptoms of their mental illness (TDMHMR Performance Contract, 2004a). Youth who appear to meet TDMHMR priority population are scheduled for an intake assessment with a Board Certified Child and Adolescent Psychiatrist or and Advanced Nurse Practitioner at the child and adolescent clinic. The licensed clinician completes a diagnostic assessment and the required Texas Department of Mental Health Mental Retardation Child and Adolescent Evaluation Assessment for Resiliency and Disease Management (CEA-RDM). Eligible youth are mostly of lower socio-economic status and either lack mental health insurance or are covered under the Children's Health Insurance Plan or Medicaid (TDMHMR Performance Contract, 2004a). Most often, the youth come from multi-problem families experiencing issues such as poverty; drug or alcohol abuse; physical abuse, sexual abuse or neglect; parental mental illness; parental incarceration; and parental criminal activity. Of all consumers served by MHMR of Tarrant County, 69% were white, 24% black, 2% Hispanic, 2% other, and 1% Asian (MHMRTC, 2005).

4.4.2 Data Collection

Data for this study was collected from the Texas Department of State Health Services computerized database. A report was pulled from the data system based on a query of study inclusion factors to identify appropriate youth that received and completed MST or usual services between September 2003 and September 2006. Included in the report were the youth's diagnostic category, age, gender, ethnicity, level of care, Ohio Problem Severity Scale scores, Ohio Functioning Scale Scores, School Behavior Scale scores, Juvenile Justice Scale scores, Family Resources Scale scores,

50

Severe Disruptive- Aggressive Behaviors Scale scores, Substance Abuse Scale scores, Risk of Self Harm Scale scores, and medication status. Youth with a level of care 2.1 received multisystemic therapy. Youth in level of care 2.2 received usual services.

4.4.3 Study Sample

From the report retrieved from the computerized data base, 87 youth who qualified for this study received MST. Eight-hundred and sixty-three youth who qualified for the study received usual services. Due to the discrepancy in numbers of eligible youth between MST and usual services, the number of youth in the MST group was categorized by ethnicity and gender. Of the youth receiving MST, 30 were African American (16 male, 14 female); 9 were Hispanic (5 male, 4 female); 47 were Caucasian (20 male, 27 female), and 1 other (female) (Table 4.1). To derive a comparison group, those who received usual services were categorized by ethnicity and gender and a stratified random sample was drawn from each category of youth to match the gender and ethnicity numbers of the MST group to enhance between group comparability (Rubin & Babbie, 2008).

Table 4.1: Study group demographics

	N	Mean Hours of Treatment	Mean Age	Gender	Ethnicity
MST Group	87	34.12	13.62	53% female 47% male	34%African American 54% Caucasian 10% Hispanic 2% Other
Usual Services Group	87	16.44	10.15	53% female 47% male	34% African American 54% Caucasian 10% Hispanic 2% Other

4.5 Independent and Dependent Variables

4.5.1 Independent Variable

4.5.1.1 Multisystemic Therapy (Treatment Group)

Multisystemic therapy (as earlier discussed in Chapter 3) was provided by a Qualified Mental Health Professional (QMHP) who received training in MST and was a licensed MST provider. MST therapists maintained a caseload of four to six families at any one time. Treatment in the MST group lasted from four to six months. Families receiving MST met with the therapist multiple times per week, sometimes daily depending on family need. Services were provided in the youth's natural environment (i.e. home, school, community). The therapist was available to the family 24 hours a day, 7 days a week. The exact nature of the therapeutic interventions varied due to the *multidetermined and multidimensional* causes of behavior problems (Henggeler et al., 1998). However, treatment focused on empowering parents, removing barriers that interfered with parental effectiveness and affecting all systems in which the youth was having difficulty (i.e. school, peer relationships) (Henggeler et al., 1998).

MST therapists received intense clinical supervision and participated in weekly phone consultation with MST Services, Inc. In addition, each therapist was monitored for fidelity with the Therapist Adherence Measure (TAM) collected from families. The MST supervisor was monitored for fidelity using the Supervisor Adherence Measure (SAM) collected from the therapists. (See Chapter 3 for detailed discussion of the TAM and SAM.)

52

4.5.1.2 Usual Services (Comparison Group)

Youth in the comparison group received the services in the TDMHMR 2.2 service package consisting of case management and family skills training using *Defiant Teen* (Barkley et al., 1999) or *Defiant Children* (Barkley, 1997). The youth/family was assigned to one of 13 Family Interventionists who received training in case management, *Defiant Teen* curriculum (Barkley et al., 1999), and *Defiant Children curriculum* (Barkley, 1997). Each of the Family Interventionists was a Qualified Mental Health Professional (QMHP).

Family Interventionists maintained a caseload of 12 to 15 families at any one time and met with the family one to two times per week for approximately 1 to 2 hours each visit. Barkley's skills training curriculums provide family training in the areas of parental management skills, parental knowledge of the social learning of childhood defiant behavior, use of positive attention and other "principle-guided parenting behavior" (Barkley et al, 1999, p. 4). Barkley (1997) developed the curriculums based on research which supports each procedure utilized throughout the manual. The skills are meant to be taught sequentially as each new skill taught is built off previous skills.

4.5.2 Dependent Variables

The measurement instrument used to answer the research questions was the Child and Adolescent Evaluation Assessment for Resiliency & Disease Management (CEA-RDM), also known as the CA-TRAG. As stated previously, each youth entering services was assessed using CA-TRAG (Texas Department of MHMR, 2004b). "The CA-TRAG was designed to provide a standardized method and a common framework for assessing the need for services and for making decisions on the level of care for children and adolescents served in the public mental health system" (Texas Department of MHMR Texas Recommended Authorization Guidelines, n.d., p.1). The CA-TRAG was administered to youth upon admission to community mental health services, upon completion of a level of care, and every 90 days while in service. The combination of diagnosis and scores on the CA-TRAG calculated the youth to a specific level of care for which he or she was eligible (service package 2.2 for this project).

The CA-TRAG consists of ratings on scores along 10 domains: the Ohio Youth Problem Severity Scale (Ogles, Lunnen, Gillespie, & Trout, 1996), the Ohio Youth Functioning Scale (Ogles et al., 1996), risk of self harm, family resources, severe disruptive or aggressive behavior, history of psychiatric treatment, co-occurring substance use, juvenile justice involvement, school behavior, and psychoactive medication treatment (See Appendix B for CA-TRAG). The two Ohio scales were completed by the parent/guardian of the youth. The clinician rated the remaining domains based on clinical assessment. The clinician rated domains were based on specific behavioral anchors that were provided for each scale to ensure consistency across clinicians and ratings. The domains were rated from 1 (no notable limitations) to 5 (extreme limitations). Table 4.2 provides an overview of components of the CA-TRAG used to test the research hypotheses.

Table 4.2: Overview of measurement instruments to test research hypotheses

Hypotheses	Scale	Rating
Overarching Hypothesis: Youth who received multisystemic therapy will experience more improved treatment outcomes than those receiving usual community services.	Ohio Problem Severity Ohio Functioning School Behavior Family Resources Risk of Self Harm Severe and Aggressive Behavior, Juvenile Justice	
1a. Youth who received multisystemic therapy will experience more improved mental health symptoms than those receiving usual community services.	Ohio Problem Severity Scale	Rated from 0 to 100 0= no symptoms noted 100 = severe symptoms
1b. Youth who received multisystemic therapy will experience more improved functioning than those receiving usual community services.	Ohio Functioning Scale	Rated from 0 to 80 0 = extreme troubles 80 = doing very well
1c. Youth who received multisystemic therapy will experience more improved school achievement than those receiving usual community services.	School Behavior Scale	1 = no problems 5 = severe problems with school
1d. Youth who received multisystemic therapy will experience more improved family relationships than those receiving usual community services.	Family Resources Scale	1 = no problems 5 = Extreme problems with youth/family relationship
1e. Youth who received multisystemic therapy will experience decreased risk of self harm than those receiving usual community services.	Risk of Self Harm Scale	1 = no risk 5 = severe risk
1f. Youth who received multisystemic therapy will experience decreased severe and aggressive behavior than those receiving usual community services.	Severe and Aggressive Behavior Scale	1 = no problems 5 = severe problems
1g. Youth who received multisystemic therapy will experience less juvenile justice involvement than those receiving usual community services.	Juvenile Justice Scale	1 = no involvement 5 = multiple arrests with at least 1 leading to adjudication

4.5.3 Reliability and Validity of Measurement Instruments

4.5.3.1 CA-TRAG

The reliability and validity of the CA-TRAG was determined using eight clinicians, a consensus panel, and a single benefit design expert (Texas Department of MHMR. *Child and Adolescent Texas recommended authorization guidelines: A study of reliability and validity,* n.d). The clinicians rated 10 case vignettes using the CA-TRAG to determine domain ratings and level of care. The case vignettes included a range of ages, ethnicities, and both male and female. The panel of experts and the single expert rater used a consensus process based on their clinical judgment to rate the vignettes. A computer program was written to calculate level of care based on domain ratings and diagnoses.

Inter-rater reliability was calculated using intra-class correlations, which averaged to $r = .87$. The criterion validity was calculated to 72.5% based on agreement between the clinicians and the consensus panel, 70% based agreement between the clinicians and the single expert, and 86.25% based on agreement between the clinicians and computer generated program. Overall, the inter-rater reliability and criterion validity were determined to be moderate. The CA-TRAG appears to have adequate validity and reliability based on the scores (Rubin and Babbie, 2004).

The study for reliability and validity had identified limitations. The small number of vignettes and use of written vignettes were both limitations. The study would have been strengthened if real life clinical situations were used rather than written vignettes. A potential for skewed results from the consensus panel is another limitation. Outcomes

56

from the consensus panel have the potential to recognize only the viewpoint of the most persuasive panel member, rather than an agreed upon consensus across panel members.

4.5.3.2 Ohio Scale

The Ohio Scale was developed to measure clinical outcomes for youth ages 5 to 18 that receive behavioral health services (Ogles, Melendez, Davis & Lunnen, 2002). The developers of the scale sought a tool that would be reliable, valid, and sensitive to change. Input from stakeholders was sought to identify the most important domains to measure. Next, several studies of children's mental health were examined to further identify important areas to include in the measurement tool. Out of those efforts, four domain areas were identified for measurement: problem severity, functioning, hopefulness, and satisfaction with services. (Due to TDMHMR only using the problem severity scale and the functioning scale in the CEA-RDM, only those two areas will be examined in depth.)

The Problem Severity Scale is a 20-item scale ranging from 0 (not at all) to 5 (all the time). The total score is calculated by summing the ratings for all the items. A higher score is correlated with more psychiatric symptoms experienced by the youth. The Functioning Scale is a 20-item questionnaire that measures the functional impairment of youth due to psychiatric symptoms. The scale ranges from 0 (extreme troubles) to 4 (doing very well). A lower score on this scale is correlated with more functional impairment experienced by the youth. To test the validity and reliability of the instrument, seven different samples, which included youth known to be experiencing mental health symptoms and youth in the community not identified as having mental health symptoms, were administered the instrument. In addition parents of youth in these groups and case mangers of the youth known to be experiencing mental health symptoms were administered the assessments.

The internal consistency of the instrument was measured using Cronbach's Alpha for each scale across the youth, parent, and worker versions for both the clinical and the comparison samples. The Problem Severity scale's internal consistency ranged from .90 to .97, which is considered a high level of internal consistency (Rubin & Babbie, 2004). The Functioning Scale was found to have internal consistency ranging from .75 to .95 across all versions, which is considered a moderate to high level of internal consistency (Rubin & Babbie, 2004).

Test-retest reliability was calculated for the youth and parent versions of the Ohio. The range of reliability found on Problem Severity Scale ranged from .72 to .88 and on the Functioning Scale it ranged from .43 to .79. The reliability was adequate or better on all measures of test-retest except for 1 youth sample. The researchers felt the location and timing of the administration of this youth sample affected its reliability. Inter-rater reliability scores were found to be adequate on the worker scale when a standardized format was used for data collection. Validity was measured by comparing the Ohio Scales to the Child and Adolescent Functional Assessment Scale, the Children's Global Assessment Scale and the Child Behavior Check List and by conducting a factor analysis. Evidence of concurrent and construct validity was found and suggested the measures of the scales assess severity of problems and youth level of functioning.

58

TDMHMR conducted its own tests for validation of the Ohio Scales (Texas Department of Mental Health Mental Retardation. *Validation and norms for the Ohio Scales among children served by the Texas Department of Mental Health and Mental Retardation*, n.d.). A total of 775 families across 12 community MHMR centers participated in the study. Of those, 536 (69%) were male, 239 (31%) were female with an average age of 12.8 (SD = 3.5). Four-hundred and seven (53%) were Hispanic, 202 (26%) White non-Hispanic, 157 (20%) African American, and 9 (1%) other. A Parent Form, Youth Form, and Worker Form were obtained on each participant for both Ohio Scales. Follow-up of 33 of the participants was completed using the same methods described above to determine the scales ability to measure change in symptoms or functioning. The researchers measured the reliability of all three scales using coefficient alpha. The coefficient alpha scores ranged from .901 to .932. The scores across all forms and all scales indicate a high level of reliability (Rubin & Babbie, 2004). Inter-correlations between all of the forms and scales ranged from .33 to .73. Overall, they were found to be systematically related with a higher relation between the Worker Forms and the Parent Forms. Thus, it was determined that the Parent Form would be the most appropriate for use in determining level of care for youth entering services with MHMR.

The amount of change in scores that indicated a statistically significant change was determined using the Standard Error of Differences. Results of the test indicated that a change of 11 points on the Problem Severity Scale indicates a statistically and clinically significant level of change. A change of 8 points on the Functioning Scale would indicate a statistically and clinically significant level of change.

Principle components of analysis were conducted to determine subscales of items for the Ohio Scales. Three sub-groups were found: internalizing symptoms, externalizing symptoms and delinquent behavior. These subscales were then correlated with the Child Behavior Check List subscales. Correlations ranged from .34 to .62. A moderately high degree of convergent validity was found between the Ohio Problem Severity Scale, but had low validity between the Ohio Functioning Scale. Pair-wise differences between the means of the CBCL and the Ohio Scales were examined across gender, age, diagnostic group, and ethnicity. No differences were found on the Parent Ohio Problem Severity Scale based on gender. Based on ethnicity, whites were found to have higher scores than Hispanics. No differences based on ethnicity were found on the Ohio Functioning Scale. Males were found to have statistically significant differences than females on the Functioning Scale. Youth ages 6 to 12 were found to have poorer functioning and symptom severity than other youth. The overall results of the study concluded that the Ohio Scales have adequate reliability, validity, and sensitivity to change.

4.5.2.4 Conclusion of Reliability and Validity of Instruments

The studies conducted by TDMHMR and the *inventors* of the Ohio Scales all point to adequate validity, reliability, and sensitivity to change of the instrument. The study of the CA-TRAG determined the instrument had overall reliability and validity.

60

As MHMR of Tarrant County was a participant in the TDMHMR studies, the CA-TRAG appears to be appropriate for use in this project.

4.6 Data Analysis

The pre and post-tests obtained from each group were compared to determine if a statistically significant change occurred across all measures and if clinically significant change occurred on the Ohio Functioning Scale and Ohio Problem Severity Scale (11 point change on the Problem Severity Scale, 8 point change on the Functioning Scale) (TDMHMR, 2003). Statistical significance means the difference in the pre-post test was not due to chance (Rubin & Babbie, 2008). Clinical significance means the improvement the youth experienced was enough to make a meaningful change whereby the youth moves from a level of dysfunction to a level of health (TDMHMR, 2003). Level of clinical significance of the other scales has not been established.

Using SPSS, paired-samples t tests and factorial multivariate analysis of covariance (MANCOVA) followed by univariate ANOVA were used to test the research hypotheses. Paired-samples t tests were used to compare the pre and post-test scores within groups across the Ohio Problem Severity Scale, Ohio Functioning Scale, School Behavior Scale, Family Resources scale, Risk of Self Harm Scale, and Severe and Aggressive Behavior Scale. Paired-samples t tests are appropriate for comparing means when the observations from the samples form pairs (Tabachnick & Fidell, 2001). In SPSS analysis, a paired samples t test was selected. For the MST group, the pre-test (intake scale) of each measurement instrument was paired with the applicable post-test (discharge scale). For instance, the intake Problem Severity Scale was entered as

61

variable 1 and the discharge problem severity scale was entered as variable 2. This was done for each of the measurement scales. Then, t scores were obtained for each and check for statistical significance. This process was then repeated for the usual services group.

MANCOVA is an appropriate statistical test when controlling for the effects of concomitant variables in a multivariate design (Tabachnick & Fidell, 2001). MANCOVA tests for a statistically significant difference between the experimental group and the comparison group after adjusting for differences among covariates, thus providing a clearer picture of the effects of the independent variables on the multiple dependent variables and a more sensitive statistical test that reduces unwanted error and improves the chances of rejecting a false null hypothesis (Tabachnick & Fidell, 2001). The pretests for the scales of the CA-TRAG were held as covariates due to lack of random assignment as it was possible the groups were not equal at pretest. Treating the pretest as a covariate removes the effects of the scores at posttest (Tabachnick & Fidell, 2001). Factorial MANCOVA is an appropriate statistical test when seeking to look at significance of group differences with multiple continuous level dependent variables, a categorical independent variable, and multiple continuous level independent variables (covariates) (Wildt & Ahtola, 1978). Age, gender, and ethnicity of study participants were treated as independent variables (covariates) to examine group differences. Factorial MANCOVA was run by selecting in SPSS under analyze, multivariate general linear model. Each of the post-tests was entered as dependent variables. Each of the pre-tests, plus the medication scale, was entered as covariates to adjust for potential

62

differences between groups on these measures. The independent variable, type of treatment was entered as a fixed factor. In addition to type of treatment; age, gender, and ethnicity of study participants were entered as fixed factors in order to treat them as independent variables (covariates) to examine group differences. Then, Factorial MANCOVA was run and an F value obtained based on treatment received. The F value was examined for significance.

A clinically significant change on the Ohio Problem Severity Scale is a drop in score from pre-test to post-test of 11 points or more (TDMHMR, 2003). To determine if a clinically significant difference occurred for each group on the Problem Severity Scale, the change from pre-test scores to post-test scores were calculated and then filtered to determine a percentage of youth who experienced a clinically significant change in score. A clinically significant change on the Ohio Functioning Scale is an increase in score from pre-test to post-test of 8 points or more (TDMHMR, 2003). To determine if a clinically significant difference occurred for each group on the Ohio Functioning Scale, scores were filtered to determine a percentage of youth who experienced a clinically significant change in score. The percentages of youth experiencing clinically significant change on each of these measures were compared across the MST and usual services groups.

Power of an experiment is the degree by which we can detect changes (Rosenthal, 2001). Power is determined by the significance level, effect size, and sample size (Rosenthal, 2001). A power level of 0.80 is considered an acceptable level of power in social science research, meaning the statistical significance test has an 80%

chance of rejection of the null hypothesis, resulting in a 20% chance of a Type II error (Rosenthal, 2001). A statistical significance level, alpha level of .05, suggests that the null hypothesis has a 0.05 or 5% probability of being true (Ruben & Babbie, 2008). An alpha level set at .05 is considered an acceptable level for social services research and is most commonly used by researchers (Rosenthal, 2001). The effect size pertains to the strength of the variables as determined by the corresponding statistics (Rosenthal, 2001). An effect size of .01 is considered small; .06 is considered medium; and over that is considered large (Cohen, 1988; Keppel, 2001). With an alpha set at .05 and an effect size set at .06 (medium), sample sizes would need to be from 40 (Cohen, 1988) to 44 for each group (Keppel, 2001). Based on available data, this study had 87 in each group for a total of 174 subjects. This sample size was large enough to have power set at .90, meaning a 90% chance of rejection of the null hypothesis (Keppel, 2001). Based on prior research of MST, it would have been optimal to set the expected effect size over .06. Unfortunately, the limited sample size of this study would not allow for that.

4.7 Internal Validity of the Study Design

Rubin and Babbie (2008) identify several threats to internal validity. These threats include history, maturation, testing, instrumental changes, statistical regression, selection biases, ambiguity about the direction of causal influence, measurement bias, research reactivity, diffusion, or imitation of treatments, compensatory equalization, compensatory rivalry, resentful demoralization, and attrition. Threats to internal validity will be discussed in relation to the study design of this proposal.

64

Having both a treatment group and comparison group helped control for threats of history and maturation. All youth in the study received pre and post-testing using the same measurement tools upon all administrations; thus, controlling for the threats of instrument changes and ambiguity about the direction of the causal influence. Pre-testing and matching ensured the MST and usual service groups' homogeneity to one another (Rubin & Babbie, 2008). Since the instruments were measuring functional impairment and symptomology, rather than measuring for a gained knowledge on part of the participants, and were administered at long intervals apart; it was not expected that *testing* was a strong threat to the internal validity of the study design.

A potential threat to the internal validity of this study centered on assessment skill of clinicians and completion of the Ohio Scales by the youth's caregiver. It was possible to have a level of measurement error due to parents completing the intake Ohio scales to ensure their child qualified for MHMR services, thus skewing the level of the initial assessment. Clinicians lacking skill to identify this as an issue might assign a youth to a level of care based on faulty measure. The addition of a comparison group helped control for this problem. Statistical regression was controlled due to all of the participants having a score in the clinical range for both the level of functioning and severity of symptoms on the Ohio Scales and having a similar level of problems with aggression, school behavior, and family resources as identified by the CA-TRAG. The overflow design, as discussed previously, reduced the possibility of selection bias.

Diffusion or imitation of treatment, compensatory equalization or rivalry, and resentful demoralization and attrition were potential threats to the internal validity of

65

this study, as all of the treatments were provided by the same MHMR center. The staff providing MST was part of a separate team located at a separate office than those providing usual services. Team meetings were held separately and clinical supervision was provided by different supervisors. Further, both groups were monitored for fidelity to their treatment modality by the MHMR of Tarrant County Quality Management Department. As previously discussed, the multisystemic therapists and supervisor were monitored for fidelity with the TAM and SAM instruments.

4.8 External Validity of Study Design

Due to the lack of random sampling, the study findings cannot be generalized past the study population. However, due to the specific fidelity requirements and program design of MST, the Texas requirement of using the CA-TRAG to determine eligibility for service packages, and the structured nature of usual services, this study could be replicated by other MHMR centers in Texas.

CHAPTER 5

STUDY FINDINGS

5.1 Introduction

The pre and post-tests obtained from each group were compared to determine if
a significant change occurred across all measures and if clinically significant change
occurred on the Ohio Functioning Scale and Ohio Problem Severity Scale. Paired-
samples t tests, factorial multivariate analysis of covariance (MANCOVA), and follow-
up univariate ANOVA were used to test the research hypotheses using the pre-post-tests
of the measurement instruments. This chapter will review the findings across each of
the scales to answer the research hypotheses and will include a discussion of findings
regarding gender, ethnicity, and age of participants.

5.2 Research Hypotheses

5.2.1 Overarching Research Hypotheses

1. Emotionally disturbed youth in a community mental health setting
with an externalizing disorder who receive multisystemic therapy will
experience more improved treatment outcomes than those receiving
usual community services.

In order to obtain a clearer picture of the effects of the independent variable on
the multiple dependent variables, a multiple analyses of covariance (MANCOVA) was

run to test the overarching research hypothesis. MANCOVA provides a more sensitive statistical test that reduces unwanted error, improves the chances of rejecting a false null hypothesis, and allows differences between more than one dependent variable to be examined while controlling for covariates (Tabachnick & Fidell, 2001). It tests for differences between the treatment group and comparison group after adjusting for differences among covariates. The pretest for the Ohio Functioning Scale, Ohio Problem Severity Scale, School Behavior Scale, Family Resource Scale, Psychotropic Medication Scale, Severe Disruptive Aggressive Behavior Scale, and Risk of Self Harm Scale were held as covariates due to lack of random assignment as it was possible the groups were not equal at pretest. Treating the pretest as a covariate removes the effects of the scores at posttest (Tabachnick & Fidell, 2001). Factorial MANCOVA was run by selecting in SPSS under analyze, multivariate general linear model. Each of the post-tests was entered as dependent variables. Each of the pre-tests, plus the medication variable, was entered as covariates to adjust for potential differences between groups on these measures. The independent variable, type of treatment was entered as a fixed factor. In addition to type of treatment; age, gender, and ethnicity of study participants were entered as fixed factors in order to treat them as independent variables (covariates) to examine group differences. Then, Factorial MANCOVA was run and a Wilks' Lambda F-value obtained based on treatment received. The F-value of Wilks' Lambda was examined for significance under the *Multivariate Tests* section of the Factorial MANCOVA output.

A significant effect with a large effect size was found (Lambda(10,154) = .851,

68

p = .005, partial η^2 = .149) for the linear combinations of all the dependent variables. A partial η^2 = .149 is considered a large effect size in social science research (Cohen, 1988; Keppel, 1991). Youth who received MST experienced a significantly higher level of improvement on the combination of school behavior, family functioning, mental health symptoms, youth functioning, juvenile justice involvement, severe aggressive - disruptive behavior, and self harm compared to youth who received usual services. This finding supports the overarching hypothesis that youth who received MST would experience more improved treatment outcomes than youth who received usual services.

Follow-up univariate ANOVAs and paired-samples t tests on each individual scale were used to test each of the secondary research hypotheses. In the Factorial MANCOVA output under the *Tests of Between-Subjects Effects*, follow-up univariate ANOVA's for each of the scales were examined to determine if a statistically significant difference existed between the MST group and usual services group on each scale. The paired-samples t tests were run to determine within group changes across each of the measurement instruments. First, in SPSS analysis, a paired samples t test was selected. For the MST group, the pre-test (intake scale) of each measurement instrument was paired with the applicable post-test (discharge scale). For instance, the intake Problem Severity Scale was entered as variable 1 and the discharge problem severity scale was entered as variable 2. This was done for each of the measurement scales. Then, t-values were obtained for each and examined for statistical significance. This process was then repeated for the usual services group. Discussions of these findings follow.

69

5.2.2 Hypothesis 1a

1a. Emotionally disturbed youth in a community mental health setting

with an externalizing disorder who receive multisystemic

therapy will experience more improved mental health symptoms

than those receiving usual community services.

5.2.2.1 Ohio Problem Severity Scale

The Ohio Problem Severity Scale was used to determine whether youth who received MST experienced more improved mental health symptoms than youth who received usual community services. The scores of the Ohio Problem Severity Scale range from 0 to 100, with 100 meaning the youth is experiencing extreme mental health symptoms and 0 meaning the youth is not experiencing any mental health symptoms.

Paired-samples t tests were run to determine whether youth in each group experienced improvement in mental health symptoms. The mean on the Ohio Problem Severity pretest for the MST group was 37.38 (sd=18.28), and the mean post-test was 27.90 (sd=16.11). A significant decrease pretest to posttest was found ($t(86)$ = 4.784, p = .000) for the MST group. The mean on the Ohio Problem Severity pretest for the usual services group was 39.33 (sd=14.88) and the mean post-test was 28.95 (sd=11.73). A significant decrease pretest to posttest was found ($t(86)$ = 5.958, p=.000) for the usual services group. Both groups were found to have significant improvement in mental health symptoms (see table 5.1). Follow-up univariate ANOVA on the Ohio Problem Severity Scale indicated that improvement on mental health symptoms was not significantly influenced by type of treatment received ($F(1,163)$ = .068, p > .05). Both

70

groups experienced a significant level of improvement. The difference in improvement

in mental health symptoms between the groups was not significant.

Table 5.1 Within group comparison of pre-post on Problem Severity Scale

Problem Severity Scale	Mean Score	Mean Change	Paired -samples t test
MST (n = 87)			
Intake	37.38		$t(86) = 4.784$
Discharge	27.90	9.483	$p = .000**$
Usual Services (n = 87)			$t(86) = 5.958$
	39.33	10.379	$p=.000**$
Intake	28.95		
Discharge			

** Statistically significant at .01 level

Table 5.2 Between groups comparison on Problem Severity Scale

Problem Severity Scale	n	Follow-up Univariate ANOVA
MST	87	
		$F(1,144) =.414$
Usual Services	87	$p > .05$

A clinically significant change in scores from pre-test to post-test is an important

factor to consider, as clinical significance means the improvement youth experienced

was enough to make a meaningful change whereby the youth moves from a level of

dysfunction to a level of health (TDMHMR, 2003). Whereas a youth can experience a

statistically significant level of improvement, this improvement does not necessarily

relate to meaningful change. A clinically significant change on the Ohio Problem

Severity Scale is a drop in score from pre-test to post-test of 11 points or more

(TDMHMR, 2003). To determine if a clinically significant difference occurred for each

group on the Problem Severity Scale, scores were filtered to determine a percentage of

71

youth who experienced a clinically significant change. Seventy-five youth across both groups experienced a clinically significant level of improvement in their mental health symptoms. Of those, 54.7 percent were from the MST group (n=41) and 45.3 percent (n=34) were from the usual services group. Univariate ANOVA indicated that level of clinically significant improvement of mental health symptoms was influenced based on treatment received (F(1,163) = 5.950, p = .016, partial η^2 = .035) (see Table 5.3). A partial η^2 = .035 is considered a small effect size (Cohen, 1988; Keppel, 1991). Though the effect size would be considered small, a significantly higher number of youth who received MST experienced a clinically significant level of improvement in mental health symptoms. Due to both groups experiencing statistically significant improvement in mental health symptoms and the MST group experiencing a statistically higher level of clinical significance, hypothesis 1a was supported.

Table 5.3 Between groups comparison of clinical significance on Problem Severity

Problem Severity Scale	% with clinical significance	Follow-up Univariate ANOVA
MST	54.7% of 75 (n= 41)	F(1, 163)=1.505
Usual Services	45.3% of 75 (n = 34)	p = .016* partial η^2 = .035

* Statistically significant at .05 level

5.2.3 Hypothesis 1b

1b. Emotionally disturbed youth in a community mental health setting with an externalizing disorder who receive multisystemic therapy will experience more improved functioning than those receiving usual community services.

72

5.2.3.1 Ohio Functioning Scale

To determine whether youth who received MST experienced more improved functioning than youth who received usual community services, a comparison between the groups was conducted using the Ohio Functioning Scale. The Ohio Functioning Scale scores range from 0 to 80, with 80 meaning the youth is not experiencing any problems with functioning and 0 meaning the youth is experiencing severe problems with functioning.

The mean on the Ohio Functioning Scale pre-test for the MST group was 38.45 (sd=14.60) and the mean post-test was 46.53 (sd=14.15). A statistically significant increase pre-test to post-test was found $(t(86) = -4.721, p = .000)$ for the MST group on the Ohio Functioning Scale. The mean on the Ohio Functioning Scale pretest for the usual services group was 36.91 (sd=15.09) and the mean post-test was 40.77 (sd=12.98). A statistically significant improvement in functioning pretest to posttest was found $(t(86) = -2.65, p = .010)$ for the usual services group. Both groups were found to have a statistically significant improvement on the Ohio Functioning Scale (Table 5.4). Univariate ANOVA comparing MST to usual services on the Ohio Functioning Scale indicated that improvement in functioning was not significantly influenced by type of treatment received $(F(1,144) = .745, p > .05)$ (Table 5.5).

Table 5.4 Within group comparison of pre-post on Ohio Functioning Scale

Ohio Functioning		Mean Score	Mean Change	Paired -samples t test
MST (n = 87)	Intake	38.45		
	Discharge	46.53	-8.080	$t(86) = -4.72$
				$p = .000**$
Usual Services				
(n = 87)	Intake	36.91	-3.862	$t(86) = -2.65$
	Discharge	40.77		$p = .010**$

** Statistically significant at .01 level

73

Table 5.5 Between groups comparison on Ohio Functioning Scale

Ohio Functioning Scale	n	Follow-up Univariate ANOVA
MST	87	
		$F(1,144) = .745$
Usual Services	87	$p > .05$

A clinically significant change on the Ohio Functioning Scale is an increase in scores from pre-test to post-test of 8 points or more. Scores were filtered to determine a percentage of youth who experienced a clinically significant change in functioning. Sixty youth were found to have experienced a clinically significant level of improvement in functioning. Of those, 57 percent (n=34) were from the MST group and 43 percent (n=26) from the usual services group. Univariate ANOVA found no significant relationship between clinical improvement in functioning and treatment received ($F(1,163) = 1.831$, $p > .05$). Due to both groups experiencing a significant level of improvement in functioning and the lack of significance between the groups, hypothesis 1b was not supported (Table 5.6).

Table 5.6 Between groups comparison of clinical significance on Functioning

Ohio Functioning Scale	% with clinical significance	Follow-up Univariate ANOVA
MST	57% of 60 (n=34)	
		$F(1,163) = 1.831$
Usual Services	43% of 60 (n = 26)	$p > .05$

5.2.4 Hypothesis 1c

1c. Emotionally disturbed youth in a community mental health setting with an externalizing disorder who receive multisystemic therapy will experience more improved school behavior than those

74

receiving usual community services.

5.2.4.1 School Behavior Scale

To determine whether youth who received MST experienced more improved school behavior than youth who received usual community services, a comparison between the groups was conducted using the School Behavior Scale. The School Behavior scores range from 1 to 5, with 1 meaning the youth is not experiencing problems in school and 5 meaning the youth is experiencing significant problems in school.

The mean on the School Behavior Scale pre-test for the MST group was 3.49 (sd=1.022), and the mean post-test was 2.85 (sd=1.343). A significant decrease pre-test to post-test was found ($t(86)$ = 5.409, p = .000) for the MST group on the School Behavior Scale. The mean pre-test for the usual services group was 3.33 (sd=1.178) and the mean post-test was 2.74 (sd=1.028). A statistically significant decrease pre-test to post-test was also found ($t(86)$ = 4.010, p = .000) for the usual services group. Follow-up univariate ANOVA on the School Behavior Scale indicated that improvement in school behavior was not significantly influenced by type of treatment received ($F(1,163)$ = .027, p > .05). Both groups were found to have a statistically significant level of improvement on the School Behavior Scale (Table 5.7); and, the difference in improvement was not due to treatment received (Table 5.8.). Thus, hypothesis 1c was not supported.

75

Table 5.7 Within group comparison of pre-post on School Behavior Scale

School Behavior Scale	Mean Score	Mean Change	Paired -samples t test
MST (n = 87)			
Intake	3.38	.69	$t(86) = 5.409$
Discharge	2.69		$p = .000**$
Usual Services			
(n = 87)	3.45	.59	$t(86) = 4.010$
Intake	2.86		$p = .000**$
Discharge			

** Statistically significant at .01 level

Table 5.8 Between groups comparison on School Behavior Scale

School Behavior Scale	n	Follow-up Univariate ANOVA
MST	87	
		$F(1,163) = .027$
Usual Services	87	$p > .05$

5.2.5 Hypothesis 1d

1d. Emotionally disturbed youth in a community mental health setting

with an externalizing disorder who receive multisystemic therapy

will experience more improved family functioning than those receiving

usual community services.

5.2.5.1 Family Resources Scale

To determine whether youth who received MST experienced more improved

family functioning than youth who received usual community services, a comparison of

the pre-post-tests was conducted using the Family Resources Scale. The Family

Resources Scale ranges from 1 to 5, with 1 meaning the family is not experiencing any

problems with relationships and resources and 5 meaning the family is experiencing

significant problems with relationships and resources. The mean pre-test for the MST

76

group was 3.20 (sd=.964) and the mean post-test was 2.78 (sd=1.156). A statistically significant decrease pretest to posttest was found (t(86) = 3.396, p = .001) for the MST group. The mean pre-test for the usual services group was 3.53 (sd=.745) and the mean post-test was 2.84 (sd=1.033). A significant decrease pre-test to post-test was also found (t(86) = 6.007, p = .000) for the usual services group. Both groups were found to have significant improvement on the Family Resources Scale (Table 5.9). Univariate ANOVA on the Family Resources Scale indicated that improvement in family functioning was not influenced by type of treatment received (F(1,163) = 1.020, p > .05) (Table 5.10). Hypothesis 1d, stating youth who received MST would experience more improved family functioning than youth who received usual services was not supported by the data.

Table 5.9 Within group comparison of pre-post on Family Resources Scale

Family Resources		Mean Score	Mean Change	Paired -samples t test
MST (n = 87)				
	Intake	3.20	.45	t(86) = 3.396
	Discharge	2.75		p = .001**
Usual Services				
(n = 87)	Intake	3.53	.66	t(86) = 6.007
	Discharge	2.87		p = .000**

** Statistically significant at .01 level

Table 5.10 Between groups comparison on Family Resources Scale

Family Resources Scale	n	Follow-up Univariate ANOVA
MST	87	
		F(1,163) = 1.020
Usual Services	87	p > .05

77

1e. Emotionally disturbed youth in a community mental health setting

with an externalizing disorder who receive multisystemic therapy

will experience decreased risk of self harm than those receiving

usual community services.

5.2.6.1 Risk of Self Harm Scale

To determine whether youth who received MST experienced a greater decrease in risk of self harm than youth who received usual community service, a comparison between the groups was conducted using the Risk of Self Harm Scale. The Risk of Self Harm Scale scores range from 1, meaning the youth is not experiencing problems with risk of self harm and 5 meaning the youth is experiencing extreme problems with risk of self harm. The mean of the Risk of Harm Scale pre-test for the MST group was 1.32 (sd=.673) and the mean post-test was 1.26 (sd=.600). A significant change pretest to posttest was not found ($t(86)$ = .689, p > .05) for the MST group. The mean on the Risk of Self Harm Scale pretest for the usual services group was 1.23 (sd=.564) and the mean post-test was 1.08 (sd=.313). A significant change pretest to posttest was found ($t(86)$ = 2.485, p = .015) for the usual services group (Table5.11). Univariate ANOVA on the Risk of Self Harm Scale indicated that improvement in self harm was not significantly influenced by type of treatment received ($F(1,163)$ = 3.39, p > .05) (5.12). As only the comparison group experienced a statistically significant level of improvement on the Risk of Self Harm Scale and the difference between groups was not significant, hypothesis 1e was not supported.

78

Table 5.11 Within group comparison of pre-post on Risk of Self Harm Scale

Risk of Self Harm Scale	Mean Score	Mean Change	Paired -samples t test
MST (n = 87)			
Intake	1.32	.057	$t(86) = .689$
Discharge	1.26		p > .05
Usual Services (n = 87)	1.23	.149	$t(86) = 2.485$
Intake	1.08		p = .015*
Discharge			

* Statistically significant at .05 level

Table 5.12 Between group comparison on Risk of Self Harm Scale

Risk of Self Harm Scale	n	Follow-up Univariate ANOVA
MST	87	
		$F(1,163) = 3.39$
Usual Services	87	p > .05

5.2.7 Hypothesis 1f

1f. Emotionally disturbed youth in a community mental health setting with an externalizing disorder who receive multisystemic therapy will experience decreased severe and aggressive behavior than those receiving usual community services.

5.2.7.1 Severe and Aggressive Behavior Scale

To determine whether youth who received MST experienced a greater decrease in severe and aggressive behavior than youth who received usual community service, a comparison between the groups was conducted using the Severe and Aggressive Behavior Scale Scale. Scores on this scale range from 1, meaning the youth is not experiencing problems with severe and aggressive behavior and 5 meaning the youth is experiencing extreme problems.

79

The mean of the Severe and Aggressive Behavior Scale pretest for the MST group was 3.36 (sd=.777) and the mean post-test was 2.69 (sd=.867). A statistically significant change pretest to posttest was found ($t(86)$ = 6.6 44, p = .000) for the MST group. The mean pretest for the usual services group was 3.47 (sd=.975) and the mean post-test was 2.86 (sd=.942). A significant change pretest to posttest was found ($t(86)$ = 5.595, p = .000) for the usual services group (Table 5.13). Univariate ANOVA on the Severe and Aggressive Behavior Scale indicated that improvement in severe and aggressive behavior was not significantly influenced by type of treatment received ($F(1,163)$ = .157, p > .05) (Table 5.14). As both groups experienced a significant level of improvement on the Severe and Aggressive Behavior Scale and the difference between groups was not significant, hypothesis 1f was not supported.

Table 5.13 Within group comparison of pre-post on Aggressive Behavior Scale

Severe and Aggressive Behavior Scale	Mean Score	Mean Change	Paired -samples t test
MST (n = 87)			
Intake	3.36	.667	$t(86)$ = 6.644
Discharge	2.69		p = .000**
Usual Services (n = 87)			
Intake	3.47	.609	$t(86)$ = 5.595
Discharge	2.86		p = .000**

** Statistically significant at .01 level

Table 5.14 Between groups comparison on Aggressive Behavior Scale

Severe and Aggressive Behavior Scale	n	Follow-up Univariate ANOVA
MST	87	
		$F(1,163)$ = .157
Usual Services	87	p > .05

5.2.8 Hypothesis 1g

1g. Emotionally disturbed youth in a community mental health setting
with a mental health Axis I externalizing disorder who receive
multisystemic therapy will experience less juvenile justice involvement
than those receiving usual community services.

5.2.8.1 Juvenile Justice Scale

At the beginning of treatment, none of the youth in either group had experienced
juvenile justice involvement. Follow-up Univariate ANOVA indicated the level of
juvenile justice involvement was affected by type of treatment received ($F(1,163) =$
5.388, $p = .022$). Youth who received MST experienced less juvenile justice
involvement than youth who received usual services, thus supporting hypothesis 1g.

5.3 Comparison by Gender, Age, and Ethnicity

Factorial MANCOVA is an appropriate statistical test when seeking to evaluate
group differences with multiple continuous level dependent variables, a categorical
independent variable, and multiple continuous level independent variables (covariates)
(Wildt & Ahtola, 1978). Age, gender, and ethnicity of study participants, as previously
discussed, were treated as independent variables (covariates) to examine the treatment
effect differences based on these variables. Multivariate analysis indicates that no
differences existed based on gender ($Lambda(6,139) = .969$, $p > .05$), ethnicity
($Lambda(6,139) = .975$, $p > .05$), or age range ($Lambda(6,139) = .922$, $p > .05$). All
participants experienced the same level of change across the scales regardless of gender,
ethnicity, or age range and type of treatment received.

81

CHAPTER 6

DISCUSSION

6.1 Introduction

This study compared multisystemic therapy to parent skills training combined with case management for emotionally disturbed youth with externalizing disorders utilizing a pretest-post-test, quasi-experimental design. This chapter will provide a discussion of study findings in relation to each of the research hypotheses followed by a discussion of study limitations. Finally, implications for social work policy, practice, and research will be discussed.

6.2 Discussion of Findings by Hypotheses

6.2.1 Overarching Research Hypotheses

Emotionally disturbed youth in a community mental health setting with

an externalizing disorder who receive multisystemic therapy

will experience more improved treatment outcomes than those receiving

usual community services.

6.2.1.1 Discussion of Overarching Research Hypothesis

The overarching research hypothesis was supported. Youth who received MST experienced more improved treatment outcomes across the combination of areas in their social ecology than youth who received usual services. The combined outcomes for school functioning, family functioning, youth functioning, youth mental health

82

symptoms, juvenile justice involvement, risk of self harm, and severe aggressive behavior were found to be significantly better for the MST group compared to the usual services group. As MST takes a social ecological approach to treating youth's problems and usual service takes a linear approach of addressing targeted youth behaviors, one would expect there to be a difference between the groups across the social ecology. From the findings, MST was more effective across the youth's social ecology than usual service thus supporting the ecological theory underscoring the MST model.

6.2.2 Hypothesis 1a

1a. Emotionally disturbed youth in a community mental health setting with

an externalizing disorder who receive multisystemic therapy will

experience more improved mental health symptoms than those

receiving usual community services.

6.2.2.1 Discussion of Hypothesis 1a

Both the MST group and usual services group experienced a significant level of improvement in the area of mental health symptoms; and, the treatments were found to be equally effective in improving mental health symptoms. While this finding differs from most MST research reporting youth who received MST experienced more improved mental health symptoms than the comparison group youth (Borduin et al., 1995; Henggeler et al., 1986; Henggeler et al., 1997; Henggeler, Rowland et al., 1999; Huey et al., 2004), it was consistent with two MST studies which reported no difference in improvement based on treatment received (Brunk et al., 1987; Henggeler, Clingempeel et al., 2002).

83

In addressing improvement in mental health symptoms, clinical significance is an important concept in determining whether improvements experienced translate into real life meaningful change. Existing MST research has not evaluated the clinical significance of change in mental health symptoms. Unlike existing MST research, this study compared the clinical level of improvement between treatment groups. While both groups were equal in improving mental health symptoms; of the youth who experienced a clinically significant level of improvement, a higher percentage was from the MST group (54.7%) than the usual services group (45.3%). Follow-up univaritate ANOVA found when comparing the level of clinically significant improvement between the groups, the MST group experienced a significantly higher level of clinical improvement in mental health symptoms than the usual service group. As questions in the literature have arisen concerning the evidence of evidence-based services (Jensen et al., 2005), clinically significant levels of improvement must be included as a factor of future research. While a treatment might provide a statistically significant level of improvement, this does not necessarily translate into a level of improvement that will affect positive change in a person's life. This again, is an important concept for future research to evaluate as clinical significance is most important in relating to true change in a youth's life.

6.2.3 Hypothesis 1b

1b. Emotionally disturbed youth in a community mental health setting with

an externalizing disorder who receive multisystemic therapy

will experience more improved functioning than those receiving usual community services.

6.2.3.1 Discussion of Hypothesis 1b

In improving youth's individual functioning, both groups experienced a significant level of improvement. This finding differs from existing MST research. All MST studies reporting on youth functioning have found those who received MST experienced more improved functioning than those who received usual services (refer to Table 1.1). The one existing study in the literature not conducted by a MST founder also found MST to be more effective than the comparison group in youth functioning (Timmons-Mitchell et al., 2006). A possible explanation in the difference of findings between this study and existing MST research could be due to this study comparing MST to another credible treatment, Defiant Teen (Barkley et al, 1999) or Child (Barkley, 1997). Other MST studies have not compared MST to treatments with any empirical support. A focus of Barkley's intervention is to improve youth behavior and functioning. While it was expected using a social ecological theoretical model would yield a higher level of youth functional improvement rather than a treatment targeting specific youth behaviors, this was not supported in this study. Both the linear focus of the comparison treatment and the social ecological focus of MST were found to be equally effective in this area.

Clinical significance is also important to evaluate when addressing youth functioning; as functioning might improve statistically, this does not necessarily translate into a level of improvement which will positively impact a youth's life. Of the youth who experienced a clinically significant level of improvement, a higher

85

percentage were from the MST group (57%) compared to the usual services group (43%). However, follow-up univariate ANOVA found the difference between the groups was not significant. Both groups were equally effective clinically. No MST studies to date have addressed clinical significance of youth functioning.

6.2.4 Hypotheses 1c, 1d, 1e, 1f

1c. Emotionally disturbed youth in a community mental health setting with an externalizing disorder who receive multisystemic therapy will experience more improved school behavior than those receiving usual community services.

1d. Emotionally disturbed youth in a community mental health setting with an externalizing disorder who receive multisystemic therapy will experience more improved family functioning than those receiving usual community services.

1e. Emotionally disturbed youth in a community mental health setting with an externalizing disorder who receive multisystemic therapy will experience decreased risk of self harm than those receiving usual community services.

1f. Emotionally disturbed youth in a community mental health setting with an externalizing disorder who receive multisystemic therapy will experience decreased severe aggressive behavior than those receiving usual community services.

6.2.4.1 Discussion of Research Hypothesis 1c, 1d, 1e, 1f

In looking individually at problems in school, problems with family functioning, and severe aggressive behavior; both the MST group and usual services group experienced significant levels of improvement in each of these areas suggesting both treatments were effective. These findings, while consistent with one MST study (Brunk et al., 1987), are not consistent with most MST research (Borduin et al., 1995; Henggeler et al., 1986; Henggeler et al., 1997; Henggeler, Rowland et al., 1999; Huey et al., 2004; Timmons-Mitchell et al., 2006). Again, a possible explanation for the difference in findings between this study and all but one of the MST studies could be due to this study comparing MST to a treatment having some empirical support (Barkley, 1997; Barkley et al., 1999). The comparison groups in MST studies supporting MST to have better outcomes received many different types of treatment with no empirical support. In the one study which did not find any differences in these areas (Brunk et al., 1987), the treatment received by the comparison group was parent behavior training, as in this study. While nothing is known about the parent behavior training in the Brunk et al, 1987 study, based on both studies, more research comparing MST to parent behavior training are warranted, as there is emerging evidence of equal effectiveness of both treatments in improving youth functioning and behavior.

6.2.5 Hypothesis 1g

1g. Emotionally disturbed youth in a community mental health setting

with an externalizing disorder who receive multisystemic therapy

will experience less juvenile justice involvement than those receiving

87

usual community services.

6.2.5.1 Discussion of Research Hypothesis 1f

The overall premise to this study was by providing an effective, culturally competent, community-based treatment to youth who have a severe emotional disturbance prior to them becoming involved with the juvenile justice system; they could be prevented from experiencing involvement. The overall reason for the development of MST was to reduce criminal behavior in youth (Henggeler, 2003). Findings of this study were consistent with the empirical literature on MST. Youth who received MST experienced less involvement in the juvenile justice system, suggesting that providing MST to seriously emotionally disturbed youth with externalizing disorders could prevent juvenile justice involvement all together. As discussed previously, many youth in the juvenile justice system end up there due to not receiving the treatment they need (Wasserman et al., 2004; Texas Institute for Policy Research, 2005). The use of MST in community mental health with this population of youth could prevent families from relinquishing custody of their children in order to receive effective treatment for them, and avert juvenile justice involvement.

6.3 Study Limitations

The findings of this study need to be viewed in context of the study limitations. This study was not as strong as the clinical trials conducted on MST due to its quasi-experimental design. Further, secondary data analysis reduced researcher control as only data collected and available by the community mental health center could be analyzed (Rubin & Babbie, 2008). Social ecological theory has been criticized for a lack of empirical evidence (Wakefield, 1996b). This was a weakness for this study as well. Available data, while measuring many areas of the youth's social ecology, did not include measures to evaluate improvement of fit across the entire social ecology and from the many perspectives across the social ecology. As each youth experienced problems of fit unique to that youth and social ecology, measures were needed to determine the level of improvement in each area identified as a problem specific to that youth. For example, if a lack of pro-social activities for the youth was identified as a driver to the youth's problems, no measure existed to determine if this area in the social ecology was improved. As MST seeks to focus interventions across the social ecology to enhance sustainability, one would expect youth receiving MST to maintain improvement across areas more so than the usual services group in which treatment was focused strictly on the individual youth. However, information on youth post-treatment was also not available to determine if one treatment sustained the improvements experienced more than the other.

The inclusion of a control group receiving no services would have enhanced the strength of this study further. However, a control group receiving no services was not available. Another way to have increased this study's strength would have been the inclusion of a control group receiving usual services at other community mental health centers. Since all of the MHMR centers in Texas use the same assessment tools and treatment modalities, this might be a possibility for future research. At the time of this study, this data was not available.

89

Another potential limitation of this study centers on assessment skill of clinicians and completion of the Ohio Scales by the youth's caregiver. It was possible to have a level of measurement error due to parents completing the intake Ohio scales to ensure their child qualified for MHMR services, thus skewing the level of the initial assessment. Clinicians lacking skill to identify this as an issue might assign a youth to a level of care based on faulty measure. The addition of a comparison group helped control for this problem.

6.4 Implications for Social Work Practice, Policy, and Research

6.4.1 Implications for Social Work Practice

There is a strong emphasis for evidence-based treatments in social work practice (Corcoran & Nichols-Casebolt, 2004). As addressed earlier, gaps exist in the empirical literature for youth with a serious emotional disturbance or co-morbidity in community mental health. Building from empirical evidence within the juvenile justice population and emerging evidence within child welfare, Multisystemic Therapy in social work practice seems to be a logical treatment modality to address the multiple needs of children and adolescents with externalizing disorders and their families in community mental health, at least for short duration.

MST addresses all the complex problems within a youth's ecological system that contribute to the youth's problems. It is not a *one-size-fits all* in-home treatment model, yet it possesses a definite structure. Treatment goals are matched to the needs and strengths of the youth and family. Criticism in family preservation and case management literature on lack of a consistent model shown to be effective is a strength

90

of MST. The strong emphasis on measuring therapist and supervisor fidelity further adds to its credibility in the literature and practice.

As social work Code of Ethics (NASW, 1999) state a social worker must, to name a few, make a commitment to the well-being of clients, intervene from a strengths perspective, provide treatment in a culturally competent manner, respect the dignity and worth of those with whom we work, and understand the importance of the relationship and engagement in effecting positive change for consumers; it is important for social workers to provide interventions consistent with these principles and values. The core principles of MST (see Appendix A) are consistent with the principles and values of the social work profession. MST interventions aimed at improving youth and family functioning are developed from the strengths of the youth, family, and social ecological system within which a youth resides. Evidence of MST effectiveness exists across many cultural, socio-economic, and racial groups.

Also consistent with social work values, MST therapists make a full commitment to their clients. A strong emphasis of MST is around therapist responsibility for engaging clients in the helping process and ensuring clients reach treatment outcomes. The MST therapist does not blame children, adolescents, or their family for not reaching goals. It is the responsibility of the therapist to engage families and ensure outcomes are met. Current evidence points to family engagement as a key element to effective treatments (Friedman, 2000). The small caseloads and availability to the family 24 hours a day, 7 days a week allow therapists more time to focus on the family, build the relationship, and engage the family in the treatment process.

91

6.4.2 Implications for Social Work Policy

A main issue in social work policy is around the cost-benefit of funding evidence-based treatments. Criticism of MST and a possible explanation of why there is a gap between the evidence of effectiveness and the lack of availability is the cost of evidence-based treatments. There is a substantial cost to implementing MST and maintaining fidelity; however, it is clearly less costly than residential treatment, not to mention the reduced cost to the juvenile justice, child welfare, or community mental health systems if outcomes are actually met and sustained. The average cost per family for MST treatment is $5000 to $6000. Medicaid case management and rehabilitation dollars can be used to offset a substantial amount of the cost. Based on practice and administrative experience, if the juvenile justice, child welfare, and mental health systems implemented MST across the systems; the cost could be further offset through sharing of consultation and supervision.

MST is a time-limited treatment, further adding to the cost savings. A typical youth and family receiving usual services will most likely receive services 6 months to several years. MST lasts an average of 3 to 6 months. MST interventions are aimed at employing the child and family with the skills and support to no longer need the system.

Policy makers need to consider the potential long-term cost-benefit, not to mention human cost-benefit of implementing evidence-based treatments such as MST. Using public dollars to pay for cheaper treatments that lack evidence could potentially result in much higher costs down the road. Following the recommendations of the New Freedom Commission to advance the uses of evidence-based services and increase the number of practitioners providing evidence-based services; with adequate funding, states could experience great strides in improving community mental health, child welfare, and juvenile justice and thus positively impact the lives of families. Further, taxpayers could realize true cost savings through avoiding the need for more costly, more restrictive levels of service. Social workers should be leaders in developing and advocating policies for the use of practices shown to be effective and consistent with social work values.

6.4.3 Implications for Social Work Research

In helping policy makers determine whether MST should be funded, the cost-benefit associated with providing MST needs to be addressed in future research. If another treatment is equally effective as MST in individual areas of a youth's life; the question of whether effectiveness of a treatment in individual areas is good enough compared to the social ecological approach of MST needs to be evaluated. Considering youth with a serious emotional disturbance in community mental health have higher co-morbidity (Weisz et al., 1998), experience multiple problems across many areas of their social ecology, and those with an externalizing disorder are the youth that tend to end up in the juvenile justice system; an argument can be made for the cost-benefit of MST. If using MST in community mental health with this population of youth will prevent the higher costs of juvenile justice involvement and the future problems in adulthood noted by Farmer et al. (2002) such as criminal activity, unemployment, inadequate parenting, relationship problems, and substance abuse; the long term costs to the youth and society will be far less. However, without a cost-benefit analysis of MST with this population

93

compared to other community-based treatments such as the one in this study; this argument cannot be made.

An increase in research conducted in the natural environment of children and adolescents with serious emotional impairments is important to increasing the knowledge base of social work and bridging the gaps of knowledge of effective community based interventions for youth and their multi-problem families. It appears from research on MST, that its strong social ecological approach, therapist responsibility to ensure family engagement and treatment outcomes, and focus of improving youth's functioning, as well as improving all systems that affect the youth; MST shows great promise in social work practice. Thus, MST research with children and adolescents in community mental health and child welfare is warranted, in addition to further research in juvenile justice. As the findings of this study showed MST to be more effective than usual services across the combination of measures, but not for each individual area, more research is needed to determine if this combined effect makes a significant difference for youth and their social ecology. Researching across all areas of the social ecology identified as drivers to a youth's problem behavior would help to bridge the lack of evidence for social ecological theory (Wakefield, 1996b). As this study found MST to be more effective than usual services in preventing juvenile justice involvement, more research on MST with seriously emotionally disturbed youth in a community mental health setting as prevention to juvenile justice involvement is needed. Demonstration projects to examine the cost-effectiveness of shared MST services across the major child serving agencies are also warranted.

MST research has had a largely male population; therefore, a focus on females is needed in future studies. Findings of this study suggest MST is equally effective for both males and females. While MST has been researched across ethnicities, Hispanic and Asian populations have been under-represented and studies have not looked at treatment differences across ethnicities. This study suggests MST is equally effective when comparing Whites and non-Whites; however, this study was not able to compare across all ethnicities due to a lack of Hispanic participants and no Asian participants. Thus, studies focusing on Hispanic and Asian populations and studies focusing on treatment outcome differences across ethnicities are needed. Though a few studies have occurred in rural settings, the majority has occurred in urban areas; thus, MST studies in rural areas are needed. Finally, studies with larger sample sizes conducted independently of MST founders are needed in addition to comparing MST to other home and community-based treatments.

Aside from continued research on MST, many other areas of research are needed to improve mental health treatment for youth with a serious emotional disturbance. The Surgeon General's Report on children's mental health (U.S. Department of Health and Human Services, 1999) identified several areas for needed research in order to improve the mental health system for children. The report recommended increased research on children's development and the correlates of serious mental health in order to develop interventions aimed at preventing serious mental health problems. The report also identified a need to support and increase research on cultural, familial, and ecological contexts in order to identify ways to promote positive mental health, reduce stigma, and improve culturally appropriate mental health treatments. Based on current literature, there exists a continued need to increase research in these areas (Dabahnah & Cooper, 2006; Gonzales, 2005; Pottick, & Warner, 2003). Research in these areas (developmental, familial, ecological and cultural contexts) could also help identify factors to improve sustainability of positive treatment effects post treatment through obtaining a greater understanding of factors that would support or impede sustainability.

While research has increased on specific treatments geared toward specific diagnoses for children (Texas Institute for Health Policy Research, 2005); other than MST, there is a lack of research on other interventions shown to be effective with multi-problem youth and families. It has been suggested in the literature that therapist characteristics are more determinant of outcomes than are client characteristics (Weisz, Donenberg, Han, & Kauneckis, 1995). This being accurate, research is needed to determine more specifically the characteristics of a therapist that lead to successful treatment outcomes and demonstration projects utilizing therapists possessing the identified characteristics and needed. Perhaps more focus on hiring therapists that possess certain skills in agencies is the most important factor to improving the mental health system.

It has also been suggested organizational factors can impede or support successful implementation of effective mental health treatments for youth (Henggeler, Schoenwald, & Pickerel, 1995). Factors include caseload size, supervision, and state of the art training. As the findings of this study were mixed, with both MST and parent training with case management being equally effective in many areas, research on a parent training/case management model with a reduced caseload and weekly supervision, as MST provides is indicated. In addition, further research is needed on organizational factors which support or impede successful implementation of a treatment.

6.5 Conclusions

It is known children's mental health problems have become more complex (Pottick & Warner, 2003). It is also known the most problematic disorders of childhood are externalizing disorders which have been associated with difficulties in adulthood (Farmer et al., 2002). Finally, it is known not providing appropriate mental health services to youth can have profound developmental consequences for children (Pottick & Warner, 2003). For these reasons, it is imperative we bring effective treatments into community mental health for youth with externalizing disorders before they reach a point of experiencing serious consequences.

This study sought to advance the knowledge of social work and contribute to filling the gaps that exist in social work research for effective, community-based mental health treatment for youth with severe emotional impairments. While findings of this study were mixed across individual areas of the youth's social ecology in that both treatments were found to be effective, the overall finding that MST improved things across the combined areas in the ecology lends support to the idea that MST may be more effective overall for serious emotionally disturbed youth with externalizing disorders than the combination of a parent behavior training and case management.

97

While MST has not been compared to this combined intervention, support for this idea exists in the literature. In a review of treatments for externalizing disorders (Farmer et al, 2002), it was noted that it is unclear if case management improves individual-level outcomes and that skills training is effective with targeted behaviors only. In contrast, MST shows support for effecting change across the social ecology (Henggeler, 2002). And, many risk factors across the social ecology contribute to the development of externalizing disorders (Stormont, 2002; Henggeler, Schoenwald et al., 2002); therefore, it is important to provide treatment that will address all of the contributing factors.

An important aspect of this study is it compared MST to another treatment with some empirical support (Barkley's skills training combined with case management), thus contributing to a need to enhance research knowledge through comparing different credible treatments to one another (Jensen et al., 2005). Another important aspect of this study is that it sought to fill the gap identified by the New Freedom Commission (2003) of a lack of culturally competent, community-based services for children and adolescents with serious emotional disturbance, to fill the gap that exists in the empirical literature of effective treatments for youth with serious emotional disturbance in community mental health (Weisz, 2000). Unlike most existing research for youth with serious emotional disturbances, the treatments in this study occurred in the homes and communities of the youth. And, as untreated or inadequately treated youth are likely to end up in the juvenile justice system, particularly those with externalizing disorders (Texas Institute for Policy Research, 2005), another strength of this study was the focus on seriously emotionally disturbed youth with externalizing disorders in an attempt to find appropriate community treatment.

As discussed earlier, other MST studies have not examined the differences of treatment effectiveness based on gender, age, or ethnicity. Because children of color living in poverty are at a higher risk of not receiving appropriate, adequate care than other youth (Gonzales, 2005), because there is a lack of research addressing girls with externalizing disorders, and because a lack of MST research on youth ages 6 to 12 exists (Farmer et al., 2002); it is important to address these factors. Using factorial MANCOVA, this study examined MST effectiveness across gender, age, and ethnicity. As stated in the findings section, MST was found to be equally effective regardless of age, ethnicity, or gender. However, the same was found for the usual services group. Both treatments appeared to be culturally competent in they were equally effective across these variables. Finally, due to current questions regarding all but one existing MST study being conducted by a founder of MST, having a study of MST conducted by an entity not connected to MST services further enhances the importance of this study.

APPENDIX A

CORE PROGRAM ELEMENTS – THE NINE CORE PRINCIPLES OF MST

CORE PROGRAM ELEMENTS - THE NINE CORE PRINCIPLES OF MST

- **Principle 1: The Primary Purpose of Assessment is to Understand the Fit Between the Identified Problems and Their Broader Systemic Context**

  The goal of MST assessment is to understand how identified problems "make sense" in light of the youth's social ecological context. Hence, the therapist integrates information obtained from family members, teachers, referral sources, and so forth to determine the factors (individual, family, peer, school, neighborhood) that are contributing to the problems, singularly or in combination. The targets of interventions are then derived from the hypotheses formulated from the assessment data. These hypotheses are subsequently confirmed or refuted through the outcomes of interventions. When hypotheses are refuted by the ineffectiveness of an intervention, the therapist seeks new information or incorporates lessons learned from the failed intervention to formulate new hypotheses and corresponding interventions. Thus, MST assessment is a reiterative process that proceeds until treatment goals are met.

  Principle 2: Therapeutic Contacts Should Emphasize the Positive and Should Use Systemic Strengths as Levers for Change

  Therapists must have the capacity to focus on the positive or families will not collaborate with treatment. Without significant family collaboration, treatment gains will be very difficult to achieve. Focusing on family strengths has numerous advantages, including: decreasing negative affect, building feelings of hope and positive expectations, identifying protective factors, decreasing frustration by emphasizing problem solving, and enhancing the caregiver's confidence. Thus, MST therapists are taught where to look for strengths and how to develop and maintain a strength-based focus.

  Principle 3: Interventions Should Be Designed to Promote Responsible Behavior and Decrease Irresponsible Behavior among Family Members

  The overriding goals of MST are to help parents and youth behave more responsibly. Parental responsibilities include providing structure and discipline, expressing love and nurturance, and meeting basic physical needs. For youth, responsible behavior includes extending effort in school, not harming others, and helping around the home. Such pragmatic conceptualizations of overriding treatment goals can be accepted by stakeholders and family members alike- which help to demystify and concretize the treatment process. Moreover, the emphasis on enhancing responsible behavior is a counterpoint to the usual pathology (e.g., conduct disorder, borderline personality disorder) focus of mental health providers and helps to engender hope for change.

  Principle 4: Interventions should be Present-Focused and Action-Oriented, Targeting Specific and Well-Defined Problems

  The purpose of this treatment principle is to encourage family transactions that are facilitating clinical progress toward unambiguous outcomes. For example, as detailed by Henggeler, Schoenwald et al. (in press), this principle enables all treatment participants to be fully aware of the direction of treatment and the criteria used to measure success. Similarly, the expectation is that family members will work actively toward meeting the goals by focusing on present-oriented solutions (versus gaining insight or focusing on the past). Clear goals also allow the therapist and family members to delineate criteria for treatment termination.

  Principle 5: Interventions should Target Sequences of Behavior within and between Multiple Systems that Maintain Identified Problems

This principle emphasizes that treatment is aimed at (a) changing family interactions in ways that promote responsible behavior and (b) promoting the family's connections with indigenous prosocial support systems including, for example, the school, competent neighbors and friends, and the church. Consistent with family systems theories of behavior, MST views changing interpersonal transactions within the child's natural environment as the key to ameliorating behavior problems (versus an emphasis on cognitive or attitudinal factors as a mechanism for behavioral change).

Principle 6: Interventions should be Developmentally Appropriate and Fit the Developmental Needs of the Youth

The nature of interventions should vary with developmental level of the youth and family. For example, in families with young adolescents who are presenting serious antisocial behavior, interventions will usually focus on developing appropriate and effective parental discipline strategies. For youth who are nearing 18 years of age, however, interventions may more appropriately focus on developing the individual youth's capacity for independence. Similarly, a developmental emphasis stresses the importance of building adolescents' competencies in peer relations and developing academic and vocational skills that will promote a successful transition to adulthood.

Principle 7: Interventions should be Designed to Require Daily or Weekly Effort by Family Members

Families referred for MST usually have extensive histories of serious problems, and our assumption is that family members and therapists must work very intensively to ameliorate these problems. In addition, the design of interventions that require ongoing efforts from multiple participants affords several therapeutic advantages (Henggeler, Schoenwald, et al., in press) including: more rapid problem resolution than obtained using less intensive interventions; timely identification of treatment non-adherence; continuous evaluation of outcomes, which enables opportunities for corrective interventions; frequent opportunities for family members to experience success and receive positive feedback; and support of family empowerment as members are orchestrating their own changes.

Principle 8: Intervention Effectiveness is Evaluated Continuously from Multiple Perspectives, with Providers Assuming Accountability for Overcoming Barriers to Successful Outcomes.

The accuracy of hypotheses concerning "fit," the efforts of family members, and the viability of interventions are evaluated based on progress toward desired outcomes. Thus, ongoing evaluation of intervention effectiveness is essential to provide timely feedback regarding these three factors (i.e., fit, effort, interventions). When interventions are producing desired results, the therapist can reasonable assume that hypotheses are accurate, family members are working, and the interventions are appropriate. On the other hand, when interventions are not producing desired results, the therapist must critically examine each of the three factors (two of which depend on the therapist's skills) and take corrective actions.

Principle 9: Interventions should be Designed to Promote Treatment Generalization and Long-Term Maintenance of Therapeutic Change by Empowering Care Givers to Address Family Members' Needs across Multiple Systemic Contexts.

Ensuring that treatment gains will generalize and be maintained when treatment ends is a critical and continuous thrust of MST interventions (Henggeler, Schoenwald, et al., in press). To facilitate these outcomes, MST aims to empower families to address current and future problems with the support of an indigenous social network of friends, neighbors, and extended family. Thus, therapists avoid "doing for" the families and stress skill building in the youth and family's natural ecology. In contrast with most mental health interventions, changes are made primarily by family members with therapists acting as consultants, advisors, and advocates.

Although these are the core treatment principles, MST is a dynamic treatment model that will always be in active refinement. For example, through randomized and quasi-experimental studies conducted by the Family Services Research Center at the Medical University of South Carolina, potential enhancements of MST are being investigated as well as modifications of MST to meet the needs of different populations (e.g., children with serious emotional disturbance, maltreated children) and service delivery models (e.g., outpatient, continuum of care). Dissemination efforts, however, will not include substantive modification of MST until such modifications have demonstrated improved outcomes.

Retrieved from: http://mstservices.com/text/treatment.html

APPENDIX B

CHILD AND ADOLESCENT RECOMMENDED ASSESSMENT GUIDELINES

(CA-TRAG)

Child and Adolescent Evaluation Assessment for Resiliency & Disease

Management (CA-TRAG)

The Child and Adolescent Evaluation Assessment for Resiliency & Disease Management form is intended to provide information about important behaviors the child has shown at the time of three separate assessments: Intake, Update, and Discharge.

Identifying Information: Complete the identifying information at the top of the form. The local case number is a maximum of 10 characters. The component code is the 3-digit TDMHMR code for your center.

Assessment Type: Indicate the type of Evaluation Assessment as **Intake**, **Update**, or **Discharge**. **Intake Non-Admission** will be automatically entered by the WebCARE screens if the purpose of the assessment is a non-admission due to ineligibility or refusal of services. If the form is for discharge, you must enter the reason that best describes the client's situation at termination (C=Level of Care services complete, J=Texas Youth Commition, N=Never returned for services within authorized service period, not to exceed 90 days, M=Moved out of local service area, T=Transferred to other community provider in local service area, Z=Other) and the date of discharge.

Intake/Annually Information:
- **Referral Source**: Enter the code of the source that first prompted or suggested the referral (1=Family/Self, 2=School, 3=Juvenile Probation, 4=TYC, 5=CPS, 6=From another division within the center - MR/SA/Emergency Services, 7=TDMHMR facility, 8=Other, 9=Unknown).
- **At Risk of Placement**: Enter **Y** if the child meets one of the following: 1) history of residential/hospital placement for mental health treatment; 2) the LAR/caregiver considers residential/hospital placement for mental health treatment a solution; or 3) the child is returning from residential/hospital placement for mental health treatment. Enter **Y** if the child meets *at least two* of the following: 1) history of school truancies; 2) history of serious alcohol/drug use; 3) history of serious behavioral problems at school; 4) history of delinquent behaviors in the community; 5) history of serious parental/caregiver rejections; and 6) history of serious behavioral problems at home.
- **ED (Special Education)**: Enter **Y** only if the child is designated special education by the school because of emotional disturbance.

Action Type: Use **Add** to add a new Evaluation Assessment form for the first time. Use **Correct/Modify** to change or add to information on a form that has been previously submitted for data entry. When using **Correct/Modify**, you must enter the identifying information exactly as it appeared on the form to be changed, then enter the correct information. Use **Delete** to delete a previously submitted form that was wrong and you want to take it out of the computer system altogether. When using **Delete**, you must enter the identifying information exactly as it appeared on the erroneous form. Therefore:
- When you want to submit the Evaluation Assessment for the first time, use **Add**.
- If you want to add to or change data on an Evaluation Assessment form that was previously submitted, use **Correct/Modify**.

Section 1: Child/Adolescent TRAG

A. Ohio Scales:
- Complete the appropriate section of the Ohio Scales (Parent, Youth, or Worker). The Ohio Scales Parent Form is preferred. Only if the parent cannot or refuses to complete the scale should an Ohio Scales Worker Form be used. The Youth Ohio scales are optional.
- For all children and adolescents, enter the Ohio Problem Severity Scale score and the Ohio Functioning Scale score.

B. CA-Texas Recommended Authorization Guidelines (TRAG) Dimension Ratings:
See the TRAG manual for instructions on completing the Rating Scales in each specified area.
- The Ohio scales (items 1 and 2) will be automatically filled from your answers in Section 1.
- For the remaining scales (3 through 9), answers must be in the range of the anchors for the 1 - 5 Likert scales. Item 10, Psychoactive Medication Treatment, has only two possible answers (**Y** or **N**).

(All dimensions must be completed.)

1. Problem Severity – Ohio Problem Severity Scale Score _____
2. Functioning – Ohio Functioning Scale Score   _____
3. Risk of Self-Harm   1 2 3 4 5
4. Severe Disruptive or Aggressive Behavior   1 2 3 4 5
5. Family Resources   1 2 3 4 5
6. History of Psychiatric Treatment   1 2 3 4 5
7. Co-occurring Substance Use   1 2 3 4 5
8. Juvenile Justice Involvement   1 2 3 4 5
9. School Behavior   1 2 3 4 5
10. Psychoactive Medication Treatment   Y N

C. Successfully Completed CA Service Package 1, 2, or 3: Indicate **Y** (Yes) or **N** (No).

D. Level of Care Decisions
Calculated Level of Care recommendation (LOC-R): This value will be calculated for you.

Calculated Level of Care Recommendation (LOC-R)   _____

E. Assessment Date: Fill in the date of the Ohio scales and TRAG in MMDDYYYY format.
Comment: Used for the name and credentials of the staff responsible for completion of this section or for provider/authority communication.

Section 2: Community Data
These items are required by the Mental Health Statistics Improvement Program (MHSIP), a federal program in which TDMHMR participates.
A. Number of Arrests in the Last 90 Days: You must complete the field for the number of arrests in the last 90 days.
B. School Days Missed in the Last 90 Days: You must complete the field for the number of scheduled school days missed in the last 90 days. Do not include school holidays and breaks when determining the number of school days missed.
C. Primary Residence Type during the Last 90 Days: You must complete the primary residence type during the last 90 days.
D. Assessment Date: Fill in the date the community data was collected in MMDDYYYY format. This section *must* be completed within 30 days of the Section 1 Assessment Date.
Comment: Used for the name and credentials of the staff responsible for completion of this section or for provider/authority communication.

Section 3: Authorized Level of Care (LOC-A) – Completed by LMHA Utilization Management LPHA staff.
A. **Actual Level of Care Authorized (LOC-A)**: Indicate the level of care that was authorized by your facility for this child.
B. **Reasons for Deviation from LOC-R**: Indicate *all the reasons* for deviation from the recommended Level of Care (LOC-R) that apply.
C. **Authorization Date**: Fill in the date the Level of Care was authorized in MMDDYYYY format. This section *must* be completed within 30 days of the Section 1 Assessment Date.
Comment: Used for the name and credentials of the staff responsible for completion of this section or for provider/authority communication.

The **Form Marked as Completed By** line should be signed by the person indicating the form is complete and ready to be entered into WebCARE. *This line is for use by the center only and will not be entered into WebCARE.*

Section 3: Authorized Level of Care (LOC-A)

A. **Actual Level of Care Authorized (LOC-A)** _____

(*Select one of the following.*)
0   = Crisis Services
1.1 = Brief Outpatient – Externalizing
1.2 = Brief Outpatient – Internalizing
2.1 = Intensive Outpatient – Multi-Systemic Therapy
2.2 = Intensive Outpatient – Externalizing
2.3 = Intensive Outpatient – Internalizing
      2.4   = Intensive Outpatient – Bipolar/Schizophrenia/Other Psychotic Disorders

3   = Treatment Foster Care
4   = Aftercare
6   = Consumer Refuses Services
8   = Waiting for All Authorized Services
9   = Not Eligible for Services

B. Reasons for Deviation from LOC-R

(*Circle all that apply.*)

Resource Limitations	Y	N
Consumer Choice	Y	N
Consumer Need	Y	N
Other	Y	N

Ohio Youth Problem, Functioning and Satisfaction Scales (Parent Form)

Child's Name: _____ Date: _____ Child's Grade: _____
Form Completed By: □ Mother □ Father □ Step-mother □ Step-father□ Other: _____

	Section I (Ohio Youth Problem Severity Scale) **Instructions:** Please rate the degree to which your child has experienced the following problems in the past 90 days.	Not at all	Once or Twice	Several Times	Often	Most of the time	All of the time
1	Arguing with others	0	1	2	3	4	5
2	Getting into fights	0	1	2	3	4	5
3	Yelling, swearing, or screaming at others	0	1	2	3	4	5
4	Fits of anger	0	1	2	3	4	5
5	Refusing to do things teachers or parents ask	0	1	2	3	4	5
6	Causing trouble for no reason	0	1	2	3	4	5
7	Using drugs or alcohol	0	1	2	3	4	5
8	Breaking rules or breaking the law (out past curfew, stealing)	0	1	2	3	4	5
9	Skipping school or classes	0	1	2	3	4	5
10	Lying	0	1	2	3	4	5
11	Can't seem to sit still, having too much energy	0	1	2	3	4	5
12	Hurting self (cutting or scratching self, taking pills)	0	1	2	3	4	5
13	Talking or thinking about death	0	1	2	3	4	5
14	Feeling worthless or useless	0	1	2	3	4	5
15	Feeling lonely and having no friends	0	1	2	3	4	5
16	Feeling anxious or fearful	0	1	2	3	4	5
17	Worrying that something bad is going to happen	0	1	2	3	4	5
18	Feeling sad or depressed	0	1	2	3	4	5
19	Nightmares	0	1	2	3	4	5
20	Eating problems	0	1	2	3	4	5

108

	Section II (Ohio Youth Functioning Scale) **Instructions**: Please rate the degree to which your child's problems affect his or her current ability in everyday activities. Consider you child's current level of functioning.	Extreme Troubles	Quite a few troubles	Some Troubles	OK	Doing Very Well
21	Getting along with friends.	0	1	2	3	4
22	Getting along with family.	0	1	2	3	4
23	Dating and developing relationships with boyfriends or girlfriends.	0	1	2	3	4
24	Getting along with adults outside the family.	0	1	2	3	4
25	Keeping neat and clean, looking good.	0	1	2	3	4
26	Caring for health needs & keeping good health habits (taking medicines/brushing teeth).	0	1	2	3	4
27	Controlling emotions and staying out of trouble.	0	1	2	3	4
28	Being motivated and finishing projects.	0	1	2	3	4
29	Participating in hobbies (baseball cards, coins, stamps, art).	0	1	2	3	4
30	Participating in recreational activities (sports, swimming, bike riding).	0	1	2	3	4
31	Completing household chores (cleaning room, other chores).	0	1	2	3	4
32	Attending school and getting passing grades in school.	0	1	2	3	4
33	Learning skills that will be useful for future jobs.	0	1	2	3	4
34	Feeling good about self.	0	1	2	3	4
35	Thinking clearly and making good decisions.	0	1	2	3	4
36	Concentrating, paying attention, and completing tasks.	0	1	2	3	4
37	Earning money and learning how to use money wisely.	0	1	2	3	4
38	Doing things without supervision or restrictions.	0	1	2	3	4
39	Accepting responsibility for actions.	0	1	2	3	4
40	Ability to express feelings.	0	1	2	3	4

Adapted from the Ohio Youth Problem, Functioning and Satisfaction Scales
Copyright © Benjamin M. Ogles & Southern Consortium for Children

Texas Department of Mental Health and Mental Retardation   September 2003 (Parent Form)

REFERENCES

American Psychiatric Association (APA). (1994). *Diagnostic and statistical manual for mental disorders* (4th ed.). Washington, DC: Author.

Anderson, H. W. (2002). Gender differences among children with externalizing behavior disorders in a clinic population. *Child Care in Practice*, 8(4), 282 – 290.

Barkley, R. A. (1997). *Defiant children: A clinician's manual for assessment and parent training* (2nd ed.). New York, NY: The Guilford Press.

Barkley, R. A., Edward, G. H., & Robin, A. L. (1999). *Defiant teens: A clinician's manual for Assessment and family intervention*. New York, NY: The Guilford Press.

Bergman, L. R., & Magnusson, D. (1997). A person-oriented approach in research on developmental psychopathology. *Developmental Psychopathology*, 9(2), 291 – 319.

Borduin, C. M., Henggeler, S. W., Blaske, D. M., & Stein, R. (1990). Multisystemic treatment of adolescent sexual offenders. *International Journal of Offender Therapy and Comparative Criminology*, 35(2), 105-114.

Borduin, C. M., Mann, B. J., Cone, L. T., Henggeler, S. W., Fucci, B. R., Blaske, D. M. et al.(1995). Multisystemic treatment of serious juvenile Offenders: Long-term prevention of criminality and violence. *Journal of Consulting and Clinical Psychology*, 63(4), 569-578.

Bronfenbrenner, U. (1979). *The ecology of human development: Experiments by nature and design*. Cambridge, MA: Harvard University Press.

110

Brown, T. L., Henggeler, S. W., Schoenwald, S. K., Brondino, M. J., & Pickerel, S.G. (1999). Multisystemic treatment of substance abusing and dependent juvenile delinquents: Effects on school attendance at post treatment and 6-month follow-up. *Children's Services: Social Policy, Research, and Practice*, 2(2), 81-93.

Brunk, M., Henggeler, S. W., & Whelan, J. P. (1987). Comparison of multisystemic therapy and parent training in brief treatment of child abuse and neglect (Electronic version). *Journal of Consulting and Clinical Psychology*, 55 (2), 171-178.

Burns, B. J., Farmer, E. M., Angold, A., Costello, E. J. & Behar, L. (1996). A randomized trial of case management for youths with serious emotional disturbance. *Journal of Clinical Child Psychology*, 25(4), 476-486.

Burns, B. J., & Friedman, R. M. (1990). Examining the research base for child mental health services and policy. *Journal of Mental Health Administration*, 17(1), 87 – 98.

Burns, B. J., & Hoagwood, K. (Eds.) (2002). *Community treatment for youth: Evidence-Based interventions for severe emotional and behavioral disorders.* New York, NY: Oxford University Press.

Burns, B. J., Hoagwood, K., & Mrazek, P. J. (1999). Effective treatment for mental disorders in children and adolescents. *Clinical Child and Family Psychology Review*, 2(4), 199-254.

Burns, B. J., Phillips, S. D., Wagner, H. R., Barth, R. P.; Kolko, D. J., Campbell, Y., & Landsverk, J. (2004). Mental health need and access to mental health services by youths involved with child welfare: A national survey. *Journal of the American Academy of Child and Adolescent Psychiatry*, 43(8), 960 – 971.

Cauce, A. M., & Morgan, C. J. (1994). Effectiveness of intensive case management for homeless adolescents: Results of a 3-month follow-up. *Journal of Emotional and Behavioral Disorders*, 2(4), 219-228.

Campbell, S. B. (1994). Hard-to-manage preschool boys: Externalizing behavior, social competence, and family context at two-year-follow-up. *Journal of Abnormal Child Psychology*, 22(2), 147 – 166.

Campbell, S. B. & Ewing, L. J. (1990). Follow-up of hard to manage preschoolers: Adjustment at age 9 and predictors of continuing symptoms. *Journal of Child Psychology and Psychiatry*, 31(6), 871 – 889.

Christensen, A., Phillips, S., Glasgow, R. E., & Johnson, S. M. (1983). Parental characteristics and interactional dysfunction in families with child behavior problems: A preliminary investigation. *Journal of Abnormal Child Psychology*, 11(1), 1573 – 2835.

Coalition for Juvenile Justice. (n.d.). Mental health needs of youth and young offenders. Issues & Facts. Retrieved December 30, 2006 from http://www.juvjustice.org/ resources/ fs002.html.

Cohen, J. (1988). *Statistical Power Analysis* (2nd ed.). Hillside, N.J.:Erlbaum.

Corcoran, J., & Nichols-Casebolt, A. (2004). Risk and resilience ecological framework for assessment and goal formulation. *Child and Adolescent Social Work Journal*, 21(3), 211-235.

Craven, P. A. & Lee, R. E. (2006). Therapeutic interventions for foster children:

    A systematic research synthesis. *Research on Social Work Practice,*

    16(3), 287 – 304.

Curtis, N. M., Ronan, K. R., & Borduin, C. M. (2004). Multisystemic treatment: A

    meta-analysis of outcome studies. *Journal of Family Psychology,* 18(3), 411-419.

Dabahnah, S. & Cooper, J. (2006). Challenges and opportunities in children's mental

    health. A view from families and youth. National Center for Children in Poverty.

    Columbia University. Retrieved April 2, 2007 from www.nccp.org.

Dixon, A., Howie, P., & Starling, J. (2004). Psychopathology in female juvenile

    offenders. *Journal of Child Psychology and Psychiatry,* 45(6), 1150 – 1158.

Dumas, J. E., Gibson, J. A., & Albin, J. B. (1989). Behavioral correlates of maternal

    depressive symptomology in conduct-disordered children. *Journal of Consulting*

    and Clinical Psychology, 57(4), 516 – 521.

Earls, F. & Carlson, M. (2001). The social ecology of child health and well-being

    (Electronic version). *Public Health,* 22(1), 143-166.

Emery, R. E. (1982). Interparental conflict and the children of discord and divorce.

    Psychological Bulletin, 92(3), 310 – 330.

Evans, M. E., & Armstrong, M. I. (1994). Development and evaluation of treatment

    foster care and family-centered intensive case management in New York.

    Journal of Emotional and Behavioral Disorders, 2(4), 228-240.

Evans, M. E., & Boothroyd, R. A. (1997). Development and implementation of an

    experimental study of the effectiveness of intensive in-home crisis services for children and their families. *Journal of Emotional & Behavioral Disorders*, 5(2), 93-106.

Evidence-based Services Committee Biennial Report. (2004). Summary of effective interventions for youth with behavioral and emotional needs. Honolulu, HI: Hawaii Department of Health, Child and Adolescent Mental Health Division.

Faraone, S. V., Biederman, J., Jetton, J. G., & Tsuang, M. T. (1997). Attention deficit disorder and conduct disorder: Longitudinal evidence of familial subtype. *Psychological Medicine*, 27(2), 291 – 300.

Farmer, E. M. Z., Compton, S. N., Burns, B. J., & Robertson, E. (2002). Review of the Evidence Base for Treatment of Childhood Psychopathology: Externalizing disorders. *Journal of Consulting and Clinical Psychology*, 70(6), 1267 – 1302.

Fergusson, D. M., Lynskey M. T., & Horwood, L. J. (1993). The effect of maternal depression on maternal ratings of child behavior. *Journal of Abnormal Child Psychology*, 21(3), 245 – 269.

Frick, P. J., Lahey, B. B., Loeber, R., Stouthamer-Loeber, M., Christ, M. A. G., & Hanson, K. (1992). Familial risk factors to oppositional defiant disorder and conduct disorder: Parental psychopathological and maternal parenting. *Journal of Consulting and Clinical Psychology*, 60, 49 – 55.

Friedman, R. M. (2000). Report of the Surgeon General's conference on children's mental health: A national action agenda. Retrieved January 1, 2001 from http://www.surgeongeneral.gov/cmh/childreport.htlm

Germain, C. B., & Bloom, M. (1999). *Human behavior in the social environment: An ecological View* (2nd ed.). New York, NY: Columbia University Press.

Gonzalez, M. J. (2005). Access to mental health services: The struggle of poverty

affected urban children of color. *Child and Adolescent Social Work Journal*, 1, 1

- 12. Retrieved December 9, 2006 from http://www.springerlink.com/media

/agxy6yxttl7kqnk3jmfk/ contributions/l/2/5/4/l2545128l03u3862.pdf

Greif, G. L. (1986). The ecosystems perspective 'meets the press.' *Social Work*, May-

June, 225-226.

Henggeler, S. W. (1999). Multisystemic therapy: An overview of clinical procedures,

outcomes, and policy implications. *Child Psychology & Psychiatry Review*,

4(1), 4-9.

Henggeler, S. W. (2003). Multisystemic therapy: an evidence-based practice for serious

clinical problems in adolescents. *Nami Beginnings*, 3: Fall, 8-10.

Henggeler, S. W. & Borduin, C. M. (1992). Multisystemic therapy adherence scales.

Unpublished instrument, Department of Psychiatry and Behavioral Sciences,

Medical University of South Carolina.

Henggeler, S. W., Clingempeel, W. G., Brondino, M. J., & Pickrel, S. G. (2002). Four-

year follow- up of multisystemic therapy with substance-abusing and substance-

dependent juvenile offenders (Electronic Version). *Journal of the American*

Academy of Child and Adolescent Psychiatry, 41(7), 868-875.

Henggeler, S. W., Halliday-Boykins, C. A., Cunningham, P. B., Randall, J., Shapiro, S.

B., & Chapman, J. E. (2006). Juvenile drug court: Enhancing outcomes by

integrating evidence-based treatments. *Journal of Consulting and Clinical*

Psychology, 74(1), 42-54.

Henggeler, S. W., Melton, G. B., Brondino, M. J., Scherer, & Hanley, J. H. (1997). Multisystemic therapy with violent and chronic juvenile offenders and their families: The role of treatment fidelity in successful dissemination. *Journal of Consulting and Clinical Psychology*, 65(5), 821-833.

Henggeler, S. W., Melton, G. B., Smith, L. A. (1992). Family preservation using Multisystemic therapy: An effective alternative to incarcerating serious Juvenile offenders (Electronic version). *Journal of Consulting and Clinical Psychology*, 60(6), 953-961.

Henggeler, S. W., Melton, G. B., Smith, L. A.; Schoenwald, S. K., & Hanley, J. H. (1993). Family preservation using multisystemic treatment: Long-term follow-up to a clinical trial with serious juvenile offenders. *Journal of Child and Family Studies*, 2(4), 283-293.

Henggeler, S. W., Pickrel, S. G. & Brondino, M. J. (1999). Multisystemic treatment of substance abusing and dependent delinquents: Outcomes, treatment fidelity, and transportability. *Mental Health Services Research*, 1(3), 171-184.

Henggeler, S. W., Rodick, J. D., Borduin, C. M., Hanson, C. L., Watson, S. M., & Urey, J. R. (1986). Multisystemic treatment of juvenile offenders: Effects on adolescent behavior and family interaction. *Developmental Psychology*, 22(1), 132-141.

Henggeler, S. W., Rowland, M. D., Halliday-Boykins, C., Sheidow, A. J., Ward, D. M., Randall, J., Pickrel, S. G., Cunningham, P. B. & Edwards, J. (2003). One-year follow-up of Multisystemic Therapy as an alternative to the hospitalization of youths in psychiatric crisis. *Journal of the American Academy of Child* and

    Adolescent Psychiatry, 42(5), 543-550.

Henggeler, S. W., Rowland, M. D., Randall, J., Ward, D. M., Pickrel, S. G.,

    Cunningham, P. B., et al. (1999). Home-based multisystemic therapy as an

    alternative to the hospitalization of youths in psychiatric Crisis: Clinical

    outcomes. *Journal of the American Academy of Child and Adolescent Psychiatry,*

    38(11), 1331-1345.

Henggeler, S. W., Schoenwald, S. K., Borduin, C. M., Rowland, M. D., & Cunningham,

    P. B. (1998). *Multisystemic treatment of antisocial behavior in children and*

    adolescents. New York, NY: The Guilford Press.

Henggeler, S. W., Schoenwald, S. K., Rowland, M. D., & Cunningham, P. B. (2002).

    Serious Emotional Disturbance in Children and Adolescents: Multisystemic

    Therapy. New York: Guilford Press.

Hill, L. G., Coie, J. D., Lochman, J. E., & Greenberg, M. T. (2004). Effectiveness of

    early screening for externalizing problems: Issues of screening accuracy and

    utility. *Journal of Consulting and Clinical Psychology,* 72(5), 809 – 820.

Hoagwood, K. (2001). Evidence-based practice in children's mental health services:

    What do we know? Why aren't we putting it to use? *Emotional and Behavioral*

    Disorders in Youth, Fall, p. 84-87.

Hoadwood, K. J. (2003). *2001-2005 Children/adolescent mental health*

    prevalence/priority population data. Retrieved July 30, 2005, from

    http://www.dshs.state.tx.us/mhreports/01-05RevisedMHChildPre-

117

PriPopData.pdf

Hoagwood, K., Burns, B. J., Kiser, L., Ringeisen, H. & Schoenwald, S. K. (2001). Evidenced-based practice in child and adolescent mental health services. *Psychiatric Services*, 59, 1179-1189.

Hudson, C.G. (2000). At the edge of chaos: A new paradigm for social work? *Journal of Social Work Education*, 36(2), 215-230.

Huey, S. J., Henggeler, S. W., Rowland, M. D., Halliday-Boykins, C. A, Cunningham, P. B., Pickrel, S.G. et al. (2004). Multisystemic therapy effects on attempted suicide by youths presenting psychiatric emergencies. *Journal of the American Academy of Child and Adolescent Psychiatry*, 43(2), 183-191.

Jensen, P.S., Weersing, R., Hoagwood, K. E., & Goldman, E. (2005). What is the evidence for evidence-based treatments? A hard look at our soft underbelly. *Mental Health Services Research*, 7(1), 53 – 74.

Kazdin, A. E., & Weisz, J. R., (1998). Identifying and developing empirically supported child and adolescent treatments. *Journal of Counseling and Clinical Psychology*, 66(1), 19-36.

Keppel, G. (1991). *Design and Analysis: A researcher's handbook* (3rd ed.). Upper Saddle River, N. J.: Prentice Hall.

Lahey, B. B., Loeber, R., Hart, E. L., Frick, P. J., Applegate, B., Zhang, Q., Green, S. M., & Russo, M. F. (1995). Four-year longitudinal study of conduct disorder in boys: Patterns and predictors of persistence. *Journal of Abnormal Psychology*, 104, 83 – 93.

Lazarus, A. A. (1996). The utility and futility of combining treatments in
psychotherapy. *Clinical Psychology*, 3(1), 59 – 68.

Lindsey, D., Martin, S. & Doh, J. (2002). The failure of intensive casework services to
reduce foster care placements: An examination of family preservation studies.
Children and Youth Services Review, 24(9/10), 743-775.

Littell, J. H., Popa, M. & Forsythe, B. (2005). Multisystemic Therapy for social,
emotional, and behavioral problems in youth aged 10 – 17. Cochrane Database
of Systematic Reviews, Issue 4, Art. No.: CD004797. DOI:
10.1002/14651858.CD004797.pub4. Retrieved December 15, 2006 from
http://www.thecochranelibary.com.

Lytton, H. & Romney, D. (1991). Parent differential socialization of boys and girls: A
meta-analysis. Psychological Bulletin, 109(22), 267 – 296.

McCallum, R. S., & Bracken, B. A. (1993). Interpersonal relations between school
children and their peers, parents, and teachers. *Educational Psychology Review*,
5(2), 1573 – 333X.

Mental Health Association in Texas (2005). Children's Mental Health Facts. Retrieved
February 1, 2007 from http://mhatexas.org /FACTSHEET Children21

Mental Health Mental Retardation of Tarrant County (2005). Annual Report. Retrieved
July 17, 2007 from www.mhmrtc.org/Doc/annual/report.pdf.

Multisystemic Therapy Services. (1998a). Multisystemic Therapy: Program Design and
Implementation. Retrieved July 10, 2005 from http://www.mstservices.com/text/
program.html.

Multisystemic Therapy Services, Inc. (1998b). Core program elements – The nine core
  principles of MST. Retrieved July 11, 2005 from http://mstservices.com
  /text/treatment.html.

National Advisory Mental Health Council Workgroup on Child and Adolescent Mental
  Health Intervention Development and Deployment. (2001). Blueprint for change:
  Research on child and adolescent mental health. Washington, D. C. Retrieved
  January 4, 2006 from http://www.nimh.nih.gov/publicat/nimhblueprint.pdf

National Association of Social Workers (1999). *Code of Ethics of the National
  Association of Social Workers.* Retrieved June 14, 2007 from
  http://www.socialworkers.org/pubs/code/code.asp

New Freedom Commission on Mental Health (2003). Achieving the promise:
  Transforming mental health care in America. Final report. DHHS Publication No.
  SMA-03-3832. Rockville, MD.

Nigg, J. T., & Hinshaw, S. P. (1998). Parent personality traits and psychopathology
  associated with antisocial behaviors in childhood attention-deficit hyperactivity
  disorder. *Journal of Child Psychology and Psychiatry,* 39(2), 145 – 159.

Nugent, W. R. (2006). The comparability of the standardized mean difference effect
  size across different measures of the same construct: Measurement
  considerations. *Educational and Psychological Measurement,* 66(4), 612-623.

Ogles, B. M., Lunnen, K. M., Gillespie D. K., & Trout, S. C. (1996). Conceptualization
  and initial development of the Ohio Scales. In C. Liberton, K. Kutash &
  Friedman, (Eds.) The 8th Annual Research Conference Proceedings, A system of

care for Children's Mental Health: Expanding the Research Base. (pp. 33-37). Tampa, FL: University of South Florida, Florida Mental Health Institute, Research and Training Center Children's Mental Health.

Ogles, B. M.; Melendez, D. G.; Davis, D. C. & Lunnen, K. M. (2000). The Ohio Youth Problem, Functioning and Satisfaction Scales: Technical Manual. Retrieved November 6, 2004, from http://oak.cats.ohiou.edu/~ogles/page1.html

Panella, D., & Henggeler, S. W. (1986). Peer interactions of conduct-disordered, anxious-withdrawn, and well-adjusted black adolescents. *Journal of Abnormal Child Psychology*, 14(1), 1573 – 2835.

Pfiffner, L. J., McBurrnett, K., Lahey, B. B., Frick, P. J., Loeber, R., Green, S., & Rathouz, P. J. (1999). Association of parental psycholpathology to the comorbid disorders of boys with attention deficit-hyperactivity disorder. *Journal of Consulting and Clinical Psychology,* 67(6), 881 – 893.

Pottick, K. J., & Warner, L. A. (2003). Nearly 66,000 youth live in U.S. mental health programs. Latest Findings in Children's Mental Health, Policy Report submitted to the Annie E. Casey Foundation. New Brunswick, N.J.: Institute for Health, Health Care Policy and Aging Research, Rutgers University, 2(1). Retrieved June 6, 2007 from http://64.233.167.104/ search?q=cache:lfwNoJybbwJ:www .dhh.louisiana.gov/offices/publications/pubs-142/Vol.%25202,%2520No. %25201%2520 %2520Summer% 25202003.pdf +Nearly+66,000+ youth+live+ in+U.S.+mental+health+ programs.+Latest+findings+in+children%27s+ mental+health&hl =en&ct=clnk&cd=1&gl=us

121

Reeves, J. C., Werry, J. S., Elkind, G. S., & Zametkin, A. (1987). Attention deficit, conduct, oppositional, and anxiety disorders in children: II. Clinical Characteristics. *Journal of American Academy of Child and Adolescent Psychiatry*, 28(6), 882 – 887.

Robins, L. N. (1991). Conduct Disorder. *Journal of Child Psychology and Psychiatry*, 32(1), 193 – 212.

Rosenthal, J. A. (2001). *Statistics and data interpretation for the helping professions*. Belmont, California: Wadsworth.

Rowland, M. D., Halliday-Boykins, C. A., Henggeler, S. W., Cunningham, P. B., Lee, G. L., Kruesi, M. J. P., & Shapiro, S. B. (2005). A randomized trial of multisystemic therapy with Hawaii's Felix Class youths. *Journal of Emotional and Behavioral Disorders*, 13(1), 13-23.

Rubin, A. & Babbie, E. R. (2004). *Research methods for social work* (5th ed.). Belmont, CA: Brooks/Cole-Thompson Learning

Rubin, A. & Babbie, E. R. (2008). *Research methods for social work* (6th ed.). Belmont, CA: Brooks/Cole-Thompson Learning

Saleebey, D. (1992). Biology's challenge to social work: Embodying the person-in - environment perspective. *Social Work*, 37(2), 112-118.

Scannapieco, M. & Connell-Carrick, K. (2005). *Child Maltreatment: An Ecological and Developmental Perspective*. New York: Oxford University Press.

Schaeffer, C. M. & Borduin, C. M. (2005). Long-term follow-up to a randomized clinical trial of Multisystemic therapy with serious and violent juvenile offenders.

Journal of Consulting and Clinical Psychology, 73(3), 445-453.

Scherer, D. G. & Brondino, M. J. (1994). Multisystemic family preservation therapy: Preliminary findings from a study of rural and minority serious adolescent offenders. *Journal of Emotional & Behavioral Disorders*, 2(4), 198-212.

Schoenwald, S. K., Henggeler, S. W., Brondino, M. J., & Rowland, M. D. (2000). Multisystemic therapy: Monitoring treatment fidelity. *Family Process*, 39(1), 83 – 103.

Schoenwald, S. K. & Rowland, M. D. (2002). Multisystemic therapy. In B. J. Burns & K. Hoagwood (Eds.), *Community treatment for youth: Evidence-based interventions for severe emotional and behavioral disorders* (pp. 91–116). New York, NY: Oxford University Press.

Stormont, M. (2002). Externalizing behavior problems in young children: Contributing factors and early intervention. *Psychology in the Schools,* 39(2), 127 – 138.

Strassberg, Z., Dodge, K. A., Bates, J. E., & Pettit, G. S. (1992). The longitudinal relation between parental conflict strategies and children's sociometric standing in kindergarten. *Merrill-Palmer Quarterly*, 38(4), 477 – 493.

Strother, K. B., Swenson, M. E., & Schoenwald, S. K. (1998). *Multisystemic therapy organizational manual.* Charleston, SC: MST Institute.

Tabachnick, B. G. & Fidell, L. S. (2001). *Using multivariate statistics* (4th ed). Boston, MA: Allyn and Bacon.

Texas Department of Mental Health Mental Retardation. (n.d.). *Child and Adolescent Texas recommended authorization guidelines: A study of reliability and validity.* Retrieved October 30, 2006, from http://www.dshs.state.tx.us/

mhprograms/RDMCAtrag.shtm

Texas Department of Mental Health Mental Retardation. (2003). *Validation and*

norms for the Ohio Scales among children served by the Texas Department

of Mental Health and Mental Retardation. Retrieved October 30, 2006, from

http://www.dshs.state.tx.us/mhprograms/RDMCAtrag.shtm

Texas Department of Mental Health and Mental Retardation Performance Contract.

(2004a). Contract between Texas Department of Mental Health and Mental

Retardation and MHMR of Tarrant County. Unpublished document.

Texas Department of Mental Health Mental Retardation. (2004b). *User's manual for*

the *child and adolescent Texas recommended authorization guidelines.*

Retrieved October 30, 2006, from http://www.dshs.state.tx.us/ mhprograms/

RDMCAtrag.shtm

Texas Institute for Health Policy Research. (2005). *Children's Mental Health Care in*

Texas: A guide to policy issues and state services. Retrieved June 12, 2005,

from http://www.healthpolicyinstitute.org/pdf_files/childrenMHReport.pdf

Texas Institute for Health Policy Research. (2003). *Children's Mental Health Care in*

Texas: Needs, Services and Funding. Retrieved September 18, 2005, from

http://www.healthpolicyinstitute.org/pdf_files/childrens_mh_hpb.pdf

Timmons-Mitchell, J., Bender, M. B., Kishna, M. A., Mitchell, C. C. (2006). An

independent effectiveness trail of multisystemic therapy with juvenile justice

youth. *Journal of Clinical Child and Adolescent Psychology,* 35(2), 227 – 236.

124

U.S. Department of Health and Human Services. Mental Health: A Report of the
    Surgeon General—Executive Summary. Rockville, MD: U.S. Department of
    Health and Human Services, Substance Abuse and Mental Health Services
    Administration, Center for Mental Health Services, National Institutes of Health,
    National Institute of Mental Health, 1999. http://www.surgeongeneral.gov
    /library/mentalhealth/summary.html

U. S. General Accounting Office. (2003). Child welfare and juvenile justice: Federal
    agencies could play a stronger role in helping states reduce the number of
    children placed solely to obtain mental health services. Retrieved December 28,
    2006 from http://www.gao.gov/highlights/d03397high.pdf

Wakefield, J. C. (1996a). Does social work need the eco-systems perspective?:
    Part 1. Is the perspective clinically useful? Social Service Review, March.

Wakefield, J. C. (1996b). Does social work need the eco-systems perspective?:
    Part 2. Does the perspective save social work from incoherence? Social Service
    Review, June.

Wasserman, G., Ko, S., & Jenson, P. (2001). Columbia guidelines for child and
    adolescent mental health referral. Emotional and Behavioral Disorders in Youth,
    23(winter), 9 – 14.

Wasserman, G. A., Ko, S. J., & Mc Reynolds, L. S. (2004). Assessing the Mental
    Health Status of Youth in Juvenile Justice Settings. Juvenile Justice Bulletin.
    Retrieved December 27, 2006 from www.ohp.usdoj.gov.

Waxman, H. A., & Collins, S. (2004). Incarceration of youth who are waiting for community mental health services in the United States. United States House of

Representatives Committee on Government Reform – Minority Staff Special

Investigations Division. Retrieved December 27, 2006 from

www.reform.house.gov/min

Webster-Stratton, C. (1996). Early-onset conduct problems: Does gender make a

difference? *Journal of Consulting and Clinical Psychology*, 64(3), 540 – 551.

Weisz, J. R., panelist (2000). *State of the evidence on treatments for children and the

research to practice gap.* Report of the Surgeon General's Conference on

Children's Mental Health: A national action agenda. Department of Health and

Human Services. Retrieved January 13, 2006, from http://www.surgeongeneral.

gov.cmh/childreport.htm

Weisz, J. R., Huey, S. J., & Weersing, V. R. (1998). Psychotherapy outcome research

with children and adolescents. *Advances in Clinical Child Psychology*, 20, 49-

91.

Wildt & Ahtola. (1978). *Analysis of Covariance.* Newbary Park, CA: Sage Publications

Zaff, J. F., Calkins, J., Bridges, L. J., & Margie, N. G. (2002). Promoting positive

mental and emotional health in teens: Some lessons from research. *Child Trends

Research Brief,* September, 1-8.